FOREWORD

This book you have in your hands, *Borden of Yale*, changed the course of my life. I read it one Sunday afternoon during a college vacation, now so many years ago, at a time when I was filled with selfish ambitions and, conversely, a list of negative goals—things I certainly did *not* want as careers. At the top of this list was being a missionary.

I was a Christian, brought up in a godly home, and anxious to serve God to the extent that his plans fit into mine.

In coming across this book in my father's library one Sunday afternoon and sitting down to read it, I came to greatly admire young Borden. He was very wealthy (which I wasn't and very much wanted to be) and, admirably, gave away large sums to philanthropic organizations. He was a dedicated Christian, spending time in personal evangelism (at which I was very poor). He was an athlete, being on the Yale wrestling team and I felt an affinity because I was on the Wheaton College wrestling team.

So, I was horrified when I learned as I read that he decided to become a missionary, leaving his high worldly opportunities. I became immensely uncomfortable as I read, realizing that he, now my hero, had taken a step that I had steadfastly refused to consider.

The climax came as I read of his going to Cairo in Egypt to become a missionary to the Muslims. Then I read that he became sick shortly afterward—and died. Something snapped

1

within me at that point and I angrily declared to God, "If that is the way You treat those who trust You and follow You, then You are not for me and I will go my own way."

Thus I stepped off the cliff, spiritually speaking, and plunged toward the rocks below.

But at that moment, God in his mercy stretched out his arm and caught me in mid-air and drew me back, for I found myself on my knees beside the chair where I had been reading this book and saying, "O God, here is my life. Take it and use it in any way you wish, even if it is being a missionary." Spiritually speaking, had it not been for this book, my life would have been a spiritual shambles.

God may not use this particular book to help you in the same way that it helped me, but by whatever means, I pray that you will come to the same conclusion I did, that the path of God is the only path for you.

Kenneth N. Taylor
Tyndale House Publishers

Borden of Yale

Mrs. Howard Taylor

BETHANY HOUSE PUBLISHERS
MINNEAPOLIS, MINNESOTA 55438
A Division of Bethany Fellowship, Inc.

Borden of Yale
Mrs. Howard Taylor

Library of Congress Catalog Card Number 88–70875
ISBN 1–55661–014–9
Copyright © 1988
All Rights Reserved

Published by Bethany House Publishers
A Division of Bethany Fellowship, Inc.
6820 Auto Club Road, Minneapolis, Minnesota 55438

Printed in the United States of America

To the mother
who loved and gave.

The life
that I now live in the flesh
I live
by the faith of the Son of God
Who loved me
and gave Himself for me.

Galatians 2:20

On the far reef the breakers
Recoil in shattered foam,
Yet still the sea behind them
Urges its forces home;
Its chant of triumph surges
Through all the thunderous din—
The wave may break in failure,
But the tide is sure to win.

O mighty sea, thy message
In changing spray is cast:
Within God's plans of progress
It matters not at last
How wide the shores of evil,
How strong the reefs of sin—
The wave may be defeated,
But the tide is sure to win.

Selected

INTRODUCTION

When word of the death of William Whiting Borden was cabled from Egypt, it was as though a wave of sorrow went round the world. There was scarcely a newspaper in the United States that did not publish some account of the life that had combined elements so unusual, and letters from many lands attested the influence of Borden's high ideals and unselfish service. It is probably true, as was stated in the *Princeton Seminary Bulletin,* that no young man of his age had ever given more to the service of God and humanity; for Borden not only gave his wealth, but himself, in a way so joyous and natural that it was manifestly a privilege rather than a sacrifice.

From Chicago, the city of his birth, came the following testimony:

A church friend of mine, working in the office of the Western Union Telegraphy Company, was much tried by the scoffings of an unbeliever concerning everything to do with religion. Whatever might be said on the other side was met with argument and denial. My friend, though an intelligent man and an earnest Christian, has little time for general reading and did not know of your son until an account of his consecrated life appeared in the daily paper. Upon reading it he at once felt that it might mean something to this unbeliever, so he laid the paper on his desk and awaited results. The scoffer read the article through, then coming to my friend said:

"I cannot understand it! There is no accounting for such a life."

He was completely silenced by the revelation of the power of God in the life your son lived. This is a small incident, Madam, but my friend has been deeply impressed and, with me, rejoices to know that Mr. Borden's biography is to be published.

A Richmond journal reaching a hundred thousand young people in the South admitted that Borden's theory of converting his many possessions of talent, vigorous strength and wealth into eternal values might not accord with the popular receipt for making the most of life.

"But," the editorial continued, "even though he was cut off in his early prime, before actually reaching his distant sphere of labor, it is doubtful whether any life of modern times has flung out to the world a more inspiring example. His investment has borne rich returns already and will continue to yield its peculiar fruit. There are thousands of talented and favored young men who will, in the light of Borden's conception of investment values, come to a new view of Christian service. Material possessions and natural gifts will be judged not by a standard of self-indulgence or worldly ambition but by their adaptability for building the Kingdom of God. Here was a fearless spirit, not chained by worldly wisdom in the disposition of his powers and possessions. Borden looked out and up, beyond all these, and grasped the really great thing of value for which to spend them."

"It was not the million dollars that came to this young American," commented another editor, "which made his life a victory and his death a world-wide call to young men and women to learn the secret of that victory. It was in things that every man can share that William Borden found the way to the life which is Christ and the death which is gain. And China and the Moslem world shall yet share that gain, as his burning torch is used to kindle in other lives the fires of a like passion for Jesus Christ."

CONTENTS

PART I

EARLY YEARS

Oh, what a glorious yoke are youth and grace, Christ and a young man!—Samuel Rutherford

It is the God-governed and not the self-governed life which counts for most, which is the best worth while.—Selected

1

ROOTED IN FAITH

Born: November 1, 1887

Out of it [the heart] are the issues of life. Prov. 4:23

To everything there is a beginning. Those who knew William Borden only in college may find it difficult to imagine him as a child. Yet, it was his childhood experiences and relationships that produced godly character in his life, making him a pure vessel fit for the Master's use. While he was a sophomore at Yale, for example, an unexpected discovery connected him in a unique way with the curly headed youth of ten years previously.

His older brother had recently married and some papers were found in preparing the Chicago home for the young couple that brought back memories of a Sunday afternoon when William was only six. As usual, Mrs. Borden had gathered her children and several nieces and nephews around her for a Scripture lesson. Before the lesson, she suggested that each should take a slip of paper and write down what they would like to be when they grew up.

This was to be done seriously. No one saw what the others had written, and after the slips were gathered they were tucked into an envelope, sealed and forgotten. When found ten years later and returned to those who had written them, the slips revealed that many dreams had come to pass. One boy had wanted to be a gentleman like his father, and one of the girls wished to travel abroad. Another desired "to help God and the soldiers of my country"—all through the First World War he was to render exceptional service. And William had written:

> I want to be an honest man when I grow up, a true and loving and kind and faithful man.

To his last day, by the grace of God, Borden had become that and much more.

William, like many boys his age loved roughhousing, excitement, and adventure. If these tended toward the dangerous side, all the better! His cousin, John Whiting, was his chief ally in escapades of all sorts. Together they attended several schools in Chicago,[1] and with another companion spent their holidays in congenial ways. It was nothing unusual for the three to start out on Saturday at five A.M., ending up at supper time completely exhausted.

One day the boys discovered that by using ropes they could travel along the roofs of the houses in Bellevue Place almost the length of the entire block. For a time this afforded them considerable amusement. Another diversion was to go down to the river and put in the day fooling around among the boats tied to the docks. They used to climb all over the boats, scaling the rigging and exploring the rest of the vessel. The noon meal they would get wherever they could, generally from the kitchen of one of the three houses.

Late one Saturday afternoon they decided that they wanted to play in the gymnasium of the school William and his friend Kelso attended even though the building was locked for the weekend. Finding the cover of a coal chute loose, they dropped in. They played around the gym until tired, then took a leisurely shower and dressed, not realizing how late it was. The boys escaped by a window which had been left unfastened. John was visiting William at the time and when they reached home at about seven-thirty, they were met by William's parents, worried and alarmed over their lateness. When the boys told of their adventure, they were promptly sent to bed with bread and

---

[1]William attended the University School and the Latin and Manual Training Schools in Chicago, before going to the Hill School, Pottstown, Pennsylvania.

milk for supper. It was meant for punishment, but nothing could have suited them better. They were exhausted and hungry, and while it was only bread and milk, the supply was unlimited.

A remarkable characteristic of William in later life was his undying commitment to doing hard tasks. Fishing, hunting, and sailing all held their excitement for the boy, but he seemed to have a love for hard jobs the best of all. When he and his cousin discovered a wreck after a terrible storm which had flooded and covered Lake Shore Drive with debris, it was important to William that they stop and help. A ship loaded with lumber had wrecked and the great timbers were lying along the shore. Seeing the work that had to be done, William and his friends were soon out in the storm, gathering up the lumber and putting it in orderly piles. A gang of Italian laborers appeared before long, but William and John Whiting kept on working, and at the end of the day lined up with the others and received their pay.

Many Saturdays and holidays were spent at their uncle's foundry some distance from Chicago. The boys never seemed to tire of this work and enjoyed working alongside the other men.

An uncle in Indiana had a farm and William would often escape there when the bitter spring winds of Chicago were too severe. While there, he was never idle, always inclined to make work his play. On one particular visit in the spring of 1898, William wanted to make cider. His uncle told him that after years of neglect the cider-press was unfit for use and could never be sufficiently cleaned. William, not to be discouraged, set out to make the machine operable once again. Ten-year-old William trudged many times up the hill for hot water, carrying his buckets two at a time. After several hours of scraping and scrubbing, the press was spotless and cider-making began.

On a visit in the spring of 1900, when he was twelve, William was up at sunrise and in the barn before the men arrived, beginning their day's work for them. This was the time he took such interest in the McKinley sawmill, going to work making strawberry boxes and stopping only after the mill whistle had blown. At the end of his visit Mr. McKinley handed him a sum of money, saying he had earned it, but William refused payment on the ground that it had been a privilege to learn.

On his last stay with his aunt and uncle on the farm in May 1912, he was the same dear, affectionate, lovable boy of old. He arrived at six in the morning. After an early breakfast, they went out to the porch. William was delighted to see the teamster, an elderly man of seventy-five who had been employed by the family for about forty years. William hailed him joyously, jumped off the porch, ran down the hill and was soon beside him on the wagon. Gently he put his arm around the old man's shoulder, and when they reached the corncrib, he took the shovel and filled the wagon with corn, driving off with him and emptying the load at its destination. He then went over to the McKinley sawmill, greeting many acquaintances and helping them in their work as in his earlier years.

His aunt will never forget the days when William, running home in his blue sweater after a day's work—rosy cheeks, eyes full of love and hair covered with shavings—called to her as he started to run up the hill, hoping he had not detained supper. She wondered if there ever was another boy so humble, with a heart so full of love and a mind thinking such pure thoughts.

Family was very important to William. He was very devoted to his mother. From the time when he played quietly in her room, so as "not to disturb her writing," when he would leave his toys and steal up behind her chair to raise the wavy hair on the back of her neck and kiss her without a word, to the days of bereavement after his father's death, when he made time in the midst of college demands and studies to write to her every day, he was more of a close friend than a son. He loved to write letters and enjoyed writing to his grandparents about the small everyday things that would happen to him.

> Elkhorn Lodge,
> Estes Park, Colorado.

Dear Grandma,

I hope you are feeling well. The third day that we were up here Papa, Mary and I went fishing over to the Big Thomson which is about half a mile south of our house, but we didn't catch anything. . . . A little while after that we went fishing again, and John caught ten but the rest of us didn't catch anything.

About 2 weeks ago, this being Tuesday the 18th, John, Mary, Ella, James and I went out after some of James's horses. We went out about 2 o'clock and we hunted the country high and low all over Beaver Flat and didn't get home until 8 o'clock, and Papa was just starting out in the buggy after us.

Now I'm going to tell you where we went and what we did. Well first we forded the Fall River and road way up into Horseshoe Park, but we didn't find the horses there, so we came back and crossed the river in a place where it was pretty deep and then we had to go through a lot of bushes which nearly swept us off our saddles. Then we crossed the ridge right near Deer Mountain. We found to get across into Beaver Flat that we had to go across a rail fence, so John took off all but one of the rails and then the horses jumped or stepped over. Well we went on and came to another rail fence and managed it in the same way. Then we came to a barbed-wire fence! Well we finally managed to pull up one of the posts and laid it down and made the horses go over, all but mine, who's name was Buckskin, and he positively refused to go over, and in trying to make him go over John backed off and pulled him onto the barbed wire and tore his pants and cut his finger.

Well, seeing my horse wouldn't go over, I had to go back and get out as best I could. . . . I then rode up into Beaver Flat about 3 miles, and was just about half way back when I met John, Ella and Mary. We went back where I'd been, only we went farther, but could not find the horses, so we went home.

On Saturday the 22nd, there was going to be a Baseball game, so we all went in the hayracks. We stopped at the Post Office and got some balls, and most everybody bought candy and gum and treated everybody to it. We got to the field which was up the Thomson a little way. They started to make the diamond. It began to rain and everybody that could got under the wagon, it stopped after a while and they practiced. I will give you a copy of the score card. . . . We won, as you see, and coming back yelled:

"Ripetake, sipetake, sis bum ba!

Elkhorn, Elkhorn, rah! rah! rah!
Who are *we?* Who are *we?*
We are the gang from James', see!"

Here I say goodbye,

Your loving grandson,
William W. Borden

It was a happy, wholesome life, and in their father the children had an understanding friend. Every night he helped them with their homework, and they knew that he was no less interested in their games and sports. He was a man of few words, but the intimacies of home life revealed the strength and nobility of his character. The following lines, written by one of his daughters upon hearing of her father's death, reveals the influence Mr. Borden had over his children.

Oh Lord, I thank Thee that Thou gavest me
This strength to cling to all my childhood years,
This noble man, my father, mine to be—
Though not as now—mine through eternity.
See, Lord! I am almost smiling through these tears,
For Thou hast made me rich of all mankind
By giving me to be his daughter-friend;
For his was calm nobility of mind
That, selfless, saw the truth and gave clear-lined
Full justice unto all things, to the end!

A sense of justice born of a pure heart
That loved a few dear ones, how sacredly!
Silent and grave, long hours he spent apart
In thought, until a word of love would start
A deep sweet look behind his eyes, and he
Would sit with us and talk from his great store,
Of beauty, poetry, and of great men.
And as the days and years opened the door
Of his dear heart to me I loved him more,
As I had more of love to give, and then—

Then, Lord, you took him from me and I wept.
It seemed so piteous, for I loved him so,
Until I fell upon my knees and crept
A little child to Thee, and wearied slept,
While quiet drifted down like cooling snow

Upon my throbbing heart. A voice then said,
"Dear child, give Me yourself and all your fears,
He now is living, loving you, now dead;
For him, for you, for this, My blood was shed."
And I awoke—strange—smiling through my tears.

William inherited some of his strongest traits through his father, who came of old Puritan stock. For the love of conquest that had taken the Bordens of Bourdonnaye to England with the Norman Duke in 1066 was followed centuries later by the love of freedom which made them exiles for conscience' sake. To exchange the rich pastures and woodlands of Kent for the barren shore and tangled forests of New England was no easy step, but Richard and John Borden, who seem to have been brothers, were driven to it by the distress of the times. The burning of heretics had ceased in their day, but ostracism and persecution were still the common lot of dissenters.

And so it came about that the first child born of European parents in Rhode Island was Matthew (1638), third son of Richard Borden. Much interesting information is available concerning the family, for at an early period they joined the Society of Friends, which keeps careful records of its members. "Glad should every Borden be that his ancestors were Quakers," writes their historian in California, and as one turns her illuminating pages, noting the contribution of generation after generation to the development of this great country, one cannot but speak highly of them.[2]

The family tended to move westward, and in the sixth generation a John Borden, who was the great-grandfather of William W. Borden, settled in Indiana.

On his mother's side, William came from a long line of soldiers, magistrates, and preachers whose histories reach into the early records of English history. The best English blood was in their veins, but the terrible years of Archbishop Laud's administration (1628–40) had driven them too far from the land they loved.

---

[2]*Historical and Genealogical Record of the Borden Family*, Hattie Borden Weld, Los Angeles, CA.

Colonel William Whiting, who brought the Whiting name to America, came with his wife Susannah from Yarmouth on the East Coast. With about a hundred others they founded the city of Hartford, Connecticut, and became members of the first church established there, under "the animated and able ministry" of the Rev. Thomas Hooker. The old records show that Whiting was "one of the civil and religious fathers of Connecticut," magistrate of the colony, and treasurer until his death. In his will he left the sum of five pounds toward mending the highways between his home and the church and no less than twenty-five pounds for his "dear and loving Pastor toward the publication of his work on the 17th of John, and any else he doth intend."

Three generations later, Charles Whiting married the beautiful Elizabeth Bradford, a descendant of Governor William Bradford of Plymouth Colony and of John Alden, who won as his bride the Puritan maiden Priscilla. The sons of Charles Whiting, who was himself a soldier, lived in the stormy days of the Revolutionary War and bore a brave part in its events. The family records pay tribute to one of them, William Bradford Whiting, by stating that he lived as "a gentleman and a Christian, an upright, honorable man, possessing great dignity of manner and such integrity of character that his very presence was a rebuke to the wicked." In middle life he moved his home from Connecticut to Canaan, a beautiful part of the state of New York, which thus became the residence of Mrs. Borden's more immediate ancestors.

Governor Bradford, "the very prop and glory of Plymouth Colony," and John Alden were thus among the ancestors of Mrs. Borden who had come to America on the *Mayflower*.

Bradford Whiting's descendants moved with the times, so the old homestead at Canaan was forsaken for regions further west. Mrs. Borden's grandfather settled in Detroit when it was little more than a village; and her father, John Talman Whiting, played an outstanding part in the development of the state of Michigan. Mrs. Borden (Mary de Garmo) was one of seven children, and passed on many of her father's lovable qualities to her son William Whiting.

But there was something more important that she passed
on to her child, for when William was about seven years old,
Mrs. Borden entered into a new spiritual experience which also
deeply affected his life. A devoted mother before, she now
became an earnest, rejoicing Christian. Christ was real to her
and fellowship with Him satisfied her beyond ordinary degree.
Instead of losing everything when she turned to Him from the
gaieties and allurements of the world, she found that she had
gained not only peace with God but a new zest for living, a
new joy in home and loved ones.

She brought new friends into the family circle; new interests
filled her life. In the Moody Church to which she transferred
her membership, she found opportunities for service as well as
the clear Bible teaching she coveted for her children. The result
was very evident in the life of her younger son, who owed the
strength and grasp of his spiritual convictions largely to that
church home.

It was there he took his first step in open confession of
Christ. Seated by his mother on a Sunday morning, he heard
Dr. R.A. Torrey, the pastor of Moody Church, give an invi-
tation to the communion service he was about to hold.

"Is it not time that you were thinking about this yourself,
William?" his mother whispered.

"I have been," was the unexpected reply.

When the elements were handed from pew to pew, to Mrs.
Borden's surprise, William quietly took the bread and wine as
did those about him. Rather taken aback at this interpretation
of her question, Mrs. Borden mentioned the matter to Dr. Torrey, who smiled and said, "Let him come and see me about it
tomorrow."

Young though he was, his answers to Dr. Torrey's questions
made it evident that he was ready for the step he had taken,
and the interview led to his joining the church.

Another important decision was made when Dr. Torrey
gave an opportunity for all who wished to dedicate their lives
to service for God to indicate this purpose by rising for prayer.
He made his meaning very plain, that it was a step of life-
consecration. William quietly rose—a little fellow in a blue

sailor-suit. He had to stand a long, long time while the service went on, but there was no wavering, and it was a consecration from which he never drew back.

Dependence upon prayer and love for the Word of God were becoming even then the daily essence of his life. "Getting off to school" was a rush for him as for other boys. He hated to be late, so he would run off with books strapped on his back and cap and lunchbox in hand. But somehow, there was always time for the little word of prayer with Mother without which the day would not have been the same. They would drop on their knees together and pray that William might know in his experience the power of the blood of Jesus Christ. That was their daily prayer in those early years, and later it was that the will of God might be done in his life.

He also loved the Word of God. Mrs. Borden never forgot what she saw one evening on going to his room when the children had returned from a delightful party. Instead of finding William undressing, he was just as he had come home, in his velvet suit with knee-breechers, pumps, and a stiff collar, seated on the edge of the bed, eagerly and serenely reading his Bible, from which he looked up at her with beaming eyes.

Later, after a journey around the world with William, his companion remarked that no matter how long a day of sight-seeing might have been, Borden never failed to close it with Bible reading and prayer. All through college and seminary it was the same. Strenuous as life was for him in his Princeton home, with all his work in theology, religious and social events, business responsibilities, and examinations ever looming in the background, his mother would find him reading in the study at the end of the evening, deep in the Book he loved, from which he would look up with the same glad light in his eyes.

2

GROUNDED IN DISCIPLINE

1902–1904

Age 14–16

Know ye not that your body is the temple of the Holy Ghost which is in you, which ye have of God, and ye are not your own? For ye are bought with a price: therefore glorify God in your body, and in your spirit, which are God's. 1 Cor. 6:19–20

—Birthday verse given to William by his mother, when he was about eight years old. It became the keynote of his life.

The glory of The Hill School when William entered it as a lad of fourteen was not its assembly hall, library, gymnasium, or athletic fields. Much of the splendid equipment of today had not yet been developed. But the school had reached notable fame through the life of its great headmaster. What he was among his boys, four hundred of whom overflowed classrooms and dining hall, may be judged from the inscription on the simple marble that marks his resting-place in the ivy-covered cloister of the chapel:

JOHN MEIGS
STRONG, IMPETUOUS, TENDER
SERVANT OF CHRIST
MASTER OF BOYS

MAKER OF MEN
HIS COURAGE WAS THE FOUNDATION OF THE
SCHOOL
HIS PASSION FOR TRUTH ITS LIGHT

"Obstacles are the glory of life," was one of his maxims,
and no slackness or shirking was tolerated at "The Hill."
"Prompt, alert, indefatigable himself, he demanded the same
of all about him," and masters as well as boys awoke under
his influence to a new stimulation, realizing what they could
accomplish. There was a buoyancy, a spirit of energetic enthusiasm that was contagious. As a headmaster wrote who had
once been on the faculty of The Hill:

"Everybody was systematically yet happily busy. There
seemed to be never an idle minute. And the background of the
picture was equally satisfying—a combination of perfectly-kept
equipment and quiet appointments, artistic taste and culture. . . . Whether in the genial, comfortable air of the diningroom, amid the varied activity of the athletic field, or in the
more rarefied atmosphere of the school-room-chapel, there was
the same heartiness and stimulus, physical, intellectual and
spiritual, and the center of it all, the animating spirit of the city
on the hill was "Professor." . . . Its ideals were his ideals and
its system was the device of his genius for making those ideals
practical and applying them to the everyday problems of life."[1]

Under the influence of Dr. Meigs, there was a splendid
insistence upon the sanctity of the body, "its reverent, radiant
uses." With all his power he sought to make his boys understand that the strength of noblest manhood is built on purity,
and that impurity is weakness and shame. "Self-reverence, self-
knowledge, self-control," he believed with Tennyson, "lead
life to sovereign power." But he was far from trusting in moral
training alone to develop the well-rounded manhood he had in
view. The following memorandum gives some of his deeper
thoughts concerning the matter: "The school must educate,
develop, guide and instruct that spiritual faculty which, by

---

[1] *The Master of the Hill,* Walter Russell Bowie, from which further quotations
are made in this chapter.

whatever name we call it, is supreme. There is no other re-straining power [than religion]. Sympathy, the innate horror of doing wrong to a fellow creature; self-respect, the innate horror of doing wrong to ourselves, are real powers in all finer natures. But a restraining power is needed. . . . The problem of school morality will be solved by a religious motive or none."

Coming from a great educator, this statement is notable, and the way in which he and his colleagues acted upon it gave a character all its own to The Hill School. The religion which John Meigs led the boys to understand and seek after was no artificial piousness, "it was a deep and manly and straightfor-ward choice of Christ as pattern and Master and Lord." In this connection he noted: "As with the aspiring athlete and the eager learner, so must it be with the young Christian. He must be taught to study the great Book of rules for daily living; to seek his great Captain in difficulty, and to ask for guidance in prayer; to heed the coach who has gained wisdom and victory in his longer game of life; and to share counsels, joy and confidences in brotherly meetings for prayer. He must realize that the test of his religious life is what he *is* and what he *does* when he is *not* on his knees in prayer, *not* reading his Bible, *not* listening to great preachers and *not* participating in religious meetings."

The Sunday services of the school held the same naturalness and appeal to William as where he lived. Distinguished preach-ers came for the regular chapel, but it was the Vesper Hour, when hymns were sung and the Professor who knew and un-derstood them best would sometimes speak and always pray what meant the most to the boys. He sat at his desk in the schoolroom for the Sunday evening song service looking firm, strong, kind, and helpful. There seemed to be something in the Professor's face as he came down the aisle at the close of those song services that the boys never quite caught at any other time, something words will not tell.

There were other things Hill boys could never forget, among them the Professor's utter sincerity and truthfulness as well as his hatred of everything mean and underhanded. They remembered that he never stole upon them unawares, but that "always his heavy footfall—every ounce of his great frame—

resounded through the corridors as he approached; and in the memory of that sound they find their most vivid impression of what is meant by the hatred of sham, subterfuge and unfairness."

He considered "truth-speaking and truth-loving the very bedrock of character," and with these he classed obedience, which in his thought stood for "willing conformity to the right standards of the school, which all must accept who accept its life": obedience not so much to rules as to "the high majesty of accepted duty." On this point he would have "no refusal and no evasion." To the father of a boy about to be expelled he wrote: "His vital and fatal lack is that of obedience. He has so indulged himself that self-pleasing is the law of his life, and deference to a higher law seems repugnant. Your . . . experience will reinforce my position touching the vital necessity of submission to law as the primal condition of moral as well as physical life and well-being."

Dr. Meigs was keenly aware also of the importance of organized games and athletics on account of the moral training they afford and their contribution to purity of life. He was fortunate in having secured the services of Michael F. Sweeney, the holder of the world's record for the high jump when Meigs came to Hill. He became not only the physical director in the gymnasium and on the track but also the coach for all the organized games. He had an excellent relationship with Dr. Meigs. Mr. Sweeney brought not only his technical skills but also the power of a Christian idealism that left a deep impression on many of the boys who would not have been reached in any other way.

Borden had come to the school well-grounded in the principles for which it stood. Sincerity and truthfulness were part of his character; one could never think of him in connection with any scheme. There was so little self-consciousness about him or morbid craving for appreciation, that one who knew him the best could say: "In all the years I was in close touch with him, I never saw him do one thing for effect."

The teachers were all cordial and William liked the Profes-

sor and Mrs. John[2] very much from what he had seen of them
so far. He had six classes, Chemistry, English, History, French,
Greek, English, and Bible History. The English Composition
was difficult. The boys had to make literal translations of parts
of Virgil or Caesar and change it in class into common English.
They were also required to write on the character of people in
the Sir Roger de Coverley papers, in the style of Steele.

William decided to take football for exercise and tried out
for the second team. He also participated in the annual interclass track meet, working with the shot put. But along with this
he loved the outdoors and hunting. In a letter to his father he
wrote:

> I wish you would get me a shot gun and give it me for my
> birthday, so that I could have it down here and shoot a little,
> so that I could go hunting at Christmas vacation.
>
> With lots of love.
> —Your son, WILLIAM

The sky was clear and cloudless, the air cool and bracing
as William headed out of the building for a walk. It had been
a good day and he was content. Algebra was easy enough to
pass. His exam in Lorna Doone was rather surprising. He had
gotten a 95. There wasn't a single mistake in spelling or punc-
tuation in the whole thing and he had not made a single mark
of correction anywhere. It was quite long, taking him nearly
two hours of steady writing.

He had to admit, however, that he was having a terribly
difficult time in studying lately, in fact he scarcely did anything

---

[2]There were two Mrs. Meigs, beloved of The Hill School—one the mother of
the Professor, who for many years had been the mainspring of its life, and the
other, "Mrs. John," who came to it as his bride in the fall of 1882. Of the
value of her contribution to the school it would be difficult to speak adequately.
"That which, joined to the influence of John Meigs himself," wrote his biographer, "more than any other thing set the tone and created the spirit of The
Hill was the touch of Mrs. Meigs upon the boys. In the lovely 'sky-parlour,'
up in the tower of the old stone building of the headmaster's house, with its
wide windows looking out over the tranquil trees, many a boy in his talks with
her had caught the gleam of new meanings for his life, going down to the
school again with the power of finer purpose in his soul."

but study every spare minute from the time he got up until school began. After lunch he had about an hour and a half spare time. Then he would begin to prepare for his afternoon lessons, and after supper start in again. By the time Saturday came about he would be so played out that it was hard to get a decent rest time in before the week began again.

The hard work, however, paid off when William's father received the following letter:

My Dear Mr. Borden

I am very happy to congratulate you on William's excellent record for the past term and to inform you that he is one of twenty members of the school who have been excused from all of their examinations.

Faithfully yours,
John Meigs

The trees were beginning to leaf and the fruit trees were in full bloom when the summer term started. William hungered for family news and some days he desired to "punch the fellow's head who sat in the mail window and said, 'Nothing for Borden,' three times a day for sometimes three and four days in succession!"

In spite of this William was having an enjoyable time playing outdoor games, baseball, track, etc. The gun club offered William an opportunity to improve his shot and he had hopes of making the gun team.

One Sunday morning, G. Campbell Morgan came and preached in the school's chapel. Some said it was one of the finest messages ever delivered there. He spoke on Mark 1:11 and 6:3: "Thou art my beloved Son, in whom I am well pleased" and "Is not this the carpenter": man's view and God's view. Pastor Morgan showed that He must have pleased God during the eighteen years that he was a carpenter. Then he went on to meditate on how much good an apprentice to Christ would have gotten. He said he did not think He would have talked of heaven or hell, but would have simply given him an example to follow by His everyday life in which there was no blemish.

Some of the fellows thought it was a little long, but William did not and wanted more. To him it was wonderful the way Morgan held everyone spellbound by his talk. For five or ten minutes no one would stir while he talked, then as if to relieve the strain he would change his tone. Then the people would shift their positions slightly and settle down again. William hoped that he would come again.

With commencement over, work began again for those who remained at the school. On Tuesday morning the swimming contests were held. Their team scratched in the relay race but finished in second place overall.

The afternoon, being a beautiful day, the interclass track meet was held. It was very close and exciting. The upperclassmen won with 43 points, William's team was second with 40. The next morning the drill was held on the field. It was not very hot and hence the drill did not seem very bad. His company did not drill very well and so did not receive the prize. Immediately following the drill, the closing exercises were held in the gym. Prizes were awarded and also gold medals. Eugene received three prizes of books for excellence in Latin, Greek, and Bible history. William was awarded one in geometry, finishing seventeenth in the school, twelfth on the second honor list and seventh in his grade.

William ate the lunch which was served right after: salmon, chicken croquettes, various salads, sandwiches, bouillon, and other tempting dishes. William took liberal portions of everything and came very near regretting it.

The following school year William again went out for football, and though he was not an outstanding player he enjoyed the challenge.

School offered studies that stretched his mind. Shortly after Christmas vacation in a letter to his mother he wrote:

> A Dr. —— was here today to preach, he was very sad. In the morning he read a thing he called the first chapter of Ephesians, but it wasn't out of the Bible and was as different as you could imagine. Then his sermon wasn't any good and was without a point. In the afternoon he didn't even try to preach a Christian sermon but gave us one from a Confucianist in

Japan. He had spent about twenty years in Japan and is quite an authority on it. This was about some fool and a class of fools, and the point was "What we had come into the world for." It was better I thought than his morning attempt, but nothing much at that. He is a teacher or something at the Union Theological Seminary. Gene thinks it the best in the country, and says practically everyone goes there to prepare for the ministry. I disagreed, and he said his grandfather had founded it. I then said that it had probably changed a great deal since that time. That man getting up there and reading his text out of some book which didn't resemble a Bible in any way, just made me tired and fixed him for me. I thought how bad things are getting to be.

I don't know whether I told you about Mr. Weed or not, but anyway he was off nearly two weeks. His mother was expected to die any moment, but she didn't and has now recovered. As a result he is feeling mighty happy and thankful. In Bible Class tonight he read about the miracle of the wine at the marriage feast. Then he said that it was the modern idea that the man who believed in miracles was way behind the times. But he said things would happen in our lives so that we would *have* to believe in them. He said, "I have seen miracles within the last two weeks and believe in them." It was good that, after some of Dr.———'s trash. I know you think the same way, and it makes me tired to hear all this talk against the old beliefs.

William was so well-grounded in the Word of God that anything that seemed to him contrary to the truth awoke an energetic reaction in his soul. Looking back on these and similar experiences, he wrote to the Committee of the Chicago Avenue Church some years later:

I am very thankful for the teaching I received at the Moody Church and Institute before I was fifteen years of age, because it kept me firm in my beliefs in spite of opposition and criticism which I was not able to answer. The great truths of the deity of Christ, His vicarious atonement, and the inspiration and authority of the Bible had been indelibly impressed upon me. I was specially impressed by the testimony of our Lord Himself to this last matter, and was willing to wait until I could go to Seminary and be prepared to meet the critics on their own ground.

Debates, orations, and the class dance were absorbing as spring came again, not to speak of the news from the Far East. William was very interested in watching the war between Russia and Japan. He would rush over to the reading room after breakfast for a glimpse at the morning papers before going to study. The newsboy who sold papers in the evening had a flourishing business because every one had to hustle to get one.

William graduated from The Hill School in 1904, receiving a grade of 83.6, fourth in a class of forty-eight boys, of whom he was the youngest.

3

OPENING EYES

1904–1905

Age 16–17

Something hidden. Go and find it. Go and look behind the Ranges—
Something lost behind the Ranges. Lost and waiting for you. Go!—R. Kipling

The war between Japan and Russia was still in progress when William Borden set out on a journey around the world in the summer of 1904. He had graduated from The Hill School at sixteen, and his parents felt that a year spent in this way would be worthwhile before he entered college. It was no small responsibility Mr. Walter Erdman had undertaken in consenting to travel with him. Scholarly, brilliant, full of humor, recently graduated from Princeton University and Seminary, a more delightful companion could hardly have been found, but his chief recommendation in Mr. and Mrs. Borden's eyes lay in his fine Christian character.

"I remember our talks about William down in the pine grove at Camden," he wrote years later, "when you were wondering what sort of companion I should make for him, and I was wondering how I could measure up to your ideals."

He remembered also Mr. Borden's helpfulness when seeing them off from Chicago. Partly in boyish bravado, William prolonged his farewells, swinging onto the train when it was already in motion.

"William," called his father sharply, "don't do things like that! It isn't fair to Mr. Erdman."

"It was a word of caution that was not forgotten," wrote the latter, "save possibly on two occasions—once when he was clambering over the fortifications of the old castle at Ajmere, and once when his familiarity with nautical matters and the management of a yacht tempted him to climb thoughtlessly on the rail and swing from the halyards of an ocean liner. The Captain administered a sharp rebuke on that occasion. William called him 'an old stiff' in private—but he came down.

"It was inevitable that a boy of his physical endowments and active disposition should be on the whole more interested in doing than in seeing things, and one does not wonder that he was more enthusiastic over a swim in the phosphorescent sea before the shrine at Kamakura than in studying the wonderful lines and graceful bulk of its great bronze Buddha. He remonstrated with me a little for being willing to see it twice! One might have supposed that so active and independent a nature would be impatient of advice or restraint. Yet, excepting the occasions mentioned, his activity never gave cause for concern, and there was no time when he failed to accept suggestions or recognize the force of another's judgment."

It was a September day when the S.S. *Korea* put out from San Francisco. Fog hung over the Golden Gate, and the departure seemed a small affair compared with the outgoing of the transatlantic liners from New York. They went down to the wharf quite early and their bags were taken up to the room by Chinese porters dressed in dark blue and round black hats with red top-knot. Their steward was a very kind Chinese man dressed like the others.

The scene at the dock was very different from the departure of an Atlantic steamer. All the servants and sailors were very competent Chinese. Men swarmed everywhere. The Chinese were by far the most interesting group to William as he observed groups of about ten squatted around pots of rice and pots of some sort of meat to eat. Each man had a little tin pan which he filled with rice. They ate by holding the pans up to their mouths while shoving in the rice with their chopsticks. They picked up pieces of meat with their chopsticks and smeared them around in a common bowl of gravy. Several of these groups were scattered across the deck and it made quite an impression.

After getting settled and having a chance to look around, William and his companion set out to meet the other passengers on board. Next to their cabin were Mr. Jones and Mr. Gibb, two young men starting out as missionaries; the same fellows that were on the train with William and Walter coming out to San Francisco. Then there was Mr. and Mrs. Lamb and their little boy. Mr. Lamb was a classmate of Walter Erdman and he and his family were going to the Philippines as missionaries. William toured the engine room with Mr. Lamb. One of the assistants also showed them the stoking rooms filled with Chinese who worked for seven dollars a month. Whenever they were hungry they set aside a few coals, built a fire on the floor, and proceeded to cook their meal. Gambling on board among the workers was done with a vengeance and they played games of chance almost every free moment.

The color of the water as it surged away from the ship was remarkable. The deep indigo blue didn't seem to be affected by the color of the sky. A day at Honolulu, where the water was clear as crystal and like melted opals in color, was welcome. Native boys, eager to dive for money, swam out to meet the ship, some of whom, scrambling on board, even dived from boats on the hurricane deck. The time passed quickly as William and Walter visited the aquarium with its rainbow-colored fish, swam, rode the surf, and drove to various points of interest until a fresh contingent of passengers came on board wearing wreaths of flowers after the custom of the island. Their journey was resumed once again.

Going around the world was quite a trip for William, but it isn't anything uncommon among the rest of the passengers. There were three or four who were on their fourth trip around, and several on their second and third. An Admiral of the U.S. Navy, a Bishop, a couple of German and Austrian Counts and

Countesses, an Italian doctor, as well as several German university students were on board.

William had spotted only one other boat since leaving San Francisco and felt the vastness of the Pacific. A strong breeze from the southeast picked up before they reached Japan. Lifelines were put up on the lower deck and all awnings taken down.

The wind developed into a gale in the afternoon and a typhoon hit its hardest during the night. It was raining hard early the next morning with the wind still blowing a gale. The Captain ordered the engines kept at half speed from 5:30 A.M. to 4:30 P.M. By that time the sea quieted down and they resumed full speed.

The next day they reached Yokohama, Japan. Japan was not the fascinating vision it would have been had they visited it in spring when the cherry and wisteria are in bloom. Fall colors touched the hills with beauty, but the people appealed more to William than the country.

Fifty years had elapsed since Commodore Perry had opened the Island Kingdom in 1853–4, and only thirty years had passed since the famous Iwakura Commission had been sent out "to survey the world and cull its best for the future development of Japan." But that brief period witnessed tremendous progress in national education, representative government, and communication. Hundreds of miles of railway connected all the important cities of the main island where previously there had been none. Schools, colleges, and universities had sprung up for the tens of thousands pursuing a modern curriculum, and the worship of the imperial line that had occupied the throne for more than two thousand years had been supplemented with parliamentary government, with a constitution granting liberty undreamed of in other Oriental lands.

Territorial expansion and increase of prestige and population had occurred side by side with all this. The war with China that had concluded ten years previously brought Formosa under the sovereignty of Japan; and the war still in progress with Russia had raised her to a first rank naval and military power. A new Japan welcomed the travelers, and yet the old was everywhere present.

The mingling of East and West was almost bewildering. In the fine train station at Yokohama, for example, the clatter of wooden clogs on the pavement was deafening, and in the narrow oriental streets it was alarming to see children playing almost under the wheels of modern vehicles. William never saw so many children before as there were in Japan. They seemed to be everywhere, in groups of four or five, sometimes more, playing in the streets. The boys and girls that ran around did not wear any socks, but rather, wooden clogs which they held with toes. Looking at them he wondered how the clogs ever stayed on. The little girls all wore kimonos, some of them in beautiful gold, red, and purple. As soon as a girl's hair was long enough, she wore it in a bunch on top of her head just like her mother's.

The boys wore the same type of clogs and kimonos as the girls but their hair was fixed differently. It was clipped quite short in a ring all around the head. Then right on top a little round spot was shaved to make it look becoming. The boys, or at least many of them, wore little soldier hats.

Many girls were running around with tiny babies tied on their backs. The babies hung there in warm weather with their little bare feet hanging out, but in the cold weather they were bundled up so that one could only see the top of their heads. The infants slept whenever they wanted and the little girls kept right on playing just the same. It was rare to see one of them crying unless she was very young or hurt. Few possessed any toys, yet they were very content.

The newspaper men, not boys, would run through the streets shouting the news, jangling bells at their waists to attract attention.

When it rained the people would carry big colorful paper umbrellas. Some of the men would wear big straw hats, and sometimes a whole suit, or a long coat made out of rice straw. William and his companion were amazed as they looked about them.

Their first railway journey was a short one, south from Yokohama to the shrines of Kamakura. At the station they took rickshaws and went first to see the Dai Butsu (a colossal statue of Buddha).[1] They approached the statue on a stone walk through a beautiful garden. The trees were so thick they could not see the statue until quite close. It was very impressive, a remarkable piece of work dating back to 1243. Around the image, foundation stones could be seen in the ground that once supported the temple that had covered the statue. It had been gone a long time, having been destroyed by a tidal wave.

From the Dai Butsu, Walter and William went to another Buddhist temple on the top of a hill overlooking the sea. This was the temple of the Goddess of Mercy, and there were many small idols around the walls. One of them was plastered with prayers on pieces of paper. These prayers had been taken from a string hung nearby. The worshiper helped himself, chewed on it a while, then threw it at the statue—if it stuck, the prayers were answered, otherwise not.

Tokyo the capital and beautiful Nikko in the mountains north of it were no disappointment. Through the kindness of a Japanese friend, they were permitted to drive through the grounds of the Palace Imperial, where Mikado, the hundred and twenty-second representative of the imperial line, lived. No other dynasty in the world approached such a record, and it was easy to understand the passionate loyalty of the people to a family of almost uniformly good rulers, which they believed to have descended from the gods.

Parliamentary government had existed for only fifteen years—"a time, no doubt, of many thrills on the part of the people, far and near, who for the first time in the nation's history were taking part in the administration of national affairs." Mikado's office was beautifully fitted out with gold-lacquer screens and a cloth of gold over the desk. The Imperial box also was very fine with such things as silks and gold lace. In various offices they saw the pictures of several Japanese

---

[1]Buddhism had been in Japan for four centuries before it became part of the national life. This colossal image of Buddha was erected to commemorate the welding together of the alien Shinto faith, first brought over by Korean missionaries, with the indigenous cult of Japan. The copper used in the construction of this magnificent image represented Shintoism while the gold represented Buddhism.

rulers. William found the room in which the representatives met was simple and unelaborate.

One morning they went to call on a Japanese lady, Mrs. Fuki O. Kami. Her house was in the suburbs of the city in a pretty, little compound. After walking through the garden they came to a house with sliding walls made of rice paper. The maid greeted them on her knees and touched her head to the floor at nearly every spoken word. While they waited, they were served tea and were then informed by their friend Mr. Hatta that they were to be received at another house, as Mrs. Kami wished to treat them as very distinguished visitors. So they walked a short distance to another little house and, after removing their shoes, they went in.

Walter had known Mrs. Kami in America, so he took the liberty of asking to be allowed to sit Japanese style instead of in the chairs offered to them. After talking a while, the maid came on her knees pushing a tray of tea and green-and-pink rice cakes before her. Mrs. Kami wore a kimono with very long sleeves. The cloth was a mixture of brown silk and old gold and was simply stunning. They had been informed that she was very wealthy, which accounted for her two homes.

In the company with Mr. Kami they arrived at a theater to see some war pictures. They checked in their shoes at the door. The floor of the theater was divided into little squares about four feet wide, and they squatted on one of these. William found the people more interesting than the pictures.

A visit to the hospital enabled them to realize something of what the war was costing day by day. They met two officers, both of whom had been terribly wounded while fighting at Port Arthur. The first one, who spoke English very well, told them a little about it. He said they were so close to the Russians that they could hear one another talking and could throw stones across. Everything in the hospital was neat, clean, and comfortable. The nurses in their white uniforms and high caps cared for the patients. Walter and William distributed appropriate Japanese gifts of flowers, books, and towels.

They continued their journey westward to the former capital of the islands, lovely Kyoto. They stopped near Mount Fuji to enjoy the hot springs of a remote valley. While they climbed through the passes, the clouds lifted and gave them a glimpse of the sacred mountain. After one climb, William wrote:

> We had a hot sulphur bath which was simply great! The Japanese tubs are made of wood and are about three feet deep and oblong in shape. Instead of climbing into them you step down. I think they are fine, and enjoy boiling in them up to my neck! I am afraid they will spoil me for any others.

To reach Nagoya they had to travel part of the way on a human-powered railroad. The car they got into was a perfect cube, measuring about five feet on each side. It was meant to seat four, but at various stages on the journey they had a number of fellow passengers. Three coolies pushed the car slowly up the hill and then jumped on while it coasted down at a terrifying rate. Just how the car stayed on the tracks going around sharp curves one could not tell, but it did.

Kyoto palaces, gardens, temples, and shops were of the finest, but they found, as Dr. Charles Erdman wrote on his later visit: "It is a city 'wholly given to idolatry.' Of course one will enjoy a visit to the grounds and buildings of the Mikado's palace; he will struggle against the temptation to bankrupt himself in the shops, which are the most attractive in the land, but his real concern in Kyoto will be with its countless temples. We rambled through acres of these, carefully depositing our shoes outside in the rain and walking in cloth slippers over vast expanses of polished floors and becoming more and more depressed by realizing the familiar fact that a proud modern empire, one of the five great powers of the world, is in the deadening grasp of false religions and degrading cults."

One of the most interesting temples that William visited was the *Sangusanguido*, the Temple of the 33,333 Gods. The building was a shabby-looking place about four hundred feet long by sixty feet wide. The images, made out of wood and gilded, all represented the same goddess: Kivanna, Goddess of Mercy. Opposite the entrance was a huge image said to be carved out of one willow tree. On either side were five hundred idols, each about five feet high. Arranged in ten rows of fifty, each row rose above the one in front of it. The images were meant to represent the eleven-faced, thousand-handed Goddess of Mercy.[2]

Of all William saw and did, there were two things that left lasting impressions. There was one picturesque letter on Japanese paper six inches wide and seven feet long in which he gives a detailed account of a sumo wrestling at Osaka, which they watched for hours. But there is another letter written to his mother that shows what his first contact with heathenism was meaning in his own life. Being in Japan less than a month, he wrote:

> Your request that I pray to God for His very best plan for my life is not a hard thing to do, for I have been praying that very thing for a long time. Although I have never thought very seriously about being a missionary until lately, I was somewhat interested in that line as you know.[3] I think this trip is going to be a great help in showing things to me in a new light. I can't explain what my views were, but I met such pleasant young people on the steamer who were going out as missionaries, and meeting them influenced me. . . .
>
> Walt has so many friends here whom we meet in nearly every city that I have seen a great deal of the work that is being done. While talking with them we learn of the work and the opportunities, etc., so that I realize things as I never did before. When I look ahead a few years it seems as though the only thing to do is to prepare for the foreign field. Of course, I want a college course and then perhaps some medical study, and certainly Bible study, at Moody Institute perhaps.
>
> I may be a little premature, but I am beginning to think a little different. I don't know what you will think of this, but anyway I know you can help me.
>
> With lots of love,
> William

---

[2]At that time, 70 percent of Japan's population (which was 78 million) was found in rural districts and they lived in 56,000 hamlets. "Scarcely any penetration has yet been made by missionary forces into this rural area. Even near Tokyo there are large districts in which the missionaries are only as one to more than a million of the population. Over 40 million, it is stated, are even today practically untouched by the Gospel. To these farmer-folk, fishermen and boatpeople, idolatry is a very sordid thing. It leaves unmet the real hunger of the heart." *The Missionary Review of the World*, October 1903. Today, 72 percent of the population of over 113 million is in the urban areas.

[3]At The Hill School, William had been chairman of the Mission Study Band.

4

VISION OF A DYING WORLD

1904–1905

Age 17

Christ has no hands but our hands to do His work today;
He has no feet but our feet to lead men in His way;
He has no tongue but our tongue to tell men how He died;
He has no help but our help to bring them to His side.

—Selected

China may not have the charm of Japan, but to William it appealed immediately. "I think I am going to like it better," he wrote, impressed with the strength and virility of the people. It was the most cosmopolitan place he had ever seen, and yet when he heard that Hong Kong was even more so, he could not fathom it.

At the bund where they landed, they were immediately introduced to several parts of Chinese culture. Of course the rickshaws were nothing new, but wheelbarrows! They were the strangest things William had ever seen. One wheel about two feet in diameter and a frame on either side for the load. A coolie had a strap from the handles that went under his arms and over his neck. Four grown people was the most they could carry, which was a heavy load. The load wasn't always balanced, making it hard on the man operating it. William, by the end of the day, mentioned to Walter that he preferred walking. The Chinese merchants as well as the foreign residents would travel up and down the bund in their carriages so that there was a continuous stream of carriages, rickshaws, and wheelbarrows. Several varieties of policemen walked the streets but the most impressive were the Sikhs with their large red turbans, thick braided beards, and immense stature. Most of them were over six or seven feet tall.

They and many other travelers stayed at the Astor House and after settling into their rooms, Walter and William went over to the China Inland Mission to consult with Mr. Stevenson on their plans for touring China. They were planning to take a river steamer to Hankow then visit Peking and other notable cities.

In mid-November the travelers boarded the steamer and traveled all day up the mouth of the Yangtze River. Immense reeds fifteen or twenty feet high grew on its banks. The river varied in width from one to seven miles and the current flowed swiftly.

It took them four days to cover the six hundred miles to Hankow. On Wednesday morning they came in sight of the city and while they were still several miles off, a number of men came out in sampans and daringly jumped on board while the steamer was going full speed. The men were the representatives of native inns eager to secure business.

Hankow had a large foreign population, as well or better equipped than the one in Shanghai. The foreign and native cities did not overlap much. Stepping through a gate from the foreign concession, William and Walter were at once plunged into the narrow dirty streets of the crowded Chinese city. Across the Yangtze was Wu Chang, a city which was larger than Hankow. On the opposite bank of the Han River, which flowed into the Yangtze at that point, was another city. The combined population of all three was about a million and a half.

Unfortunately, instead of traveling extensively in China, William was soon confined to a sick bed in a hospital. He did, however, get in two weeks in the Yangtze Valley, including a wonderful time at Nanking where they were guests of Dr. Stewart of the American Methodist College. They had crossed the Pacific with these friends and were delighted to see them again. William missed the companionship of people his own age, but it is safe to say that the Ming tombs did not suffer in interest through the companionship they had at Nanking. In this connection he wrote:

> I have come to the conclusion that young people of either sex never travel out here and in fact don't exist! I almost feel as though we were breaking the rules. We have met scarcely any young people. There were two fellows and two or three girls on the *Korea*, no more. In Japan, none. However, we hope for better things. . . .

In the early part of December, William was ill with fever. When they reached Canton it was diagnosed as typhoid. This added seriously to Mr. Erdman's responsibilities, who was thankful to get him safely to the hospital on Victoria Peak overlooking the city and harbor of Hong Kong. Fortunately the illness proved to be a mild attack and William was soon convalescent. Although in bed, he managed to pass the time very well, reading a good deal: magazines, interesting books, and his Bible. Now and then he was able to read an American paper as well.

They stayed in Canton four days and were able to tour quite a bit of it. They were able to see this fascinating city carried about the narrow streets in comfortable chairs by three bearers. The open shops were captivating, varying in width from about twenty feet, in residential areas, to six or seven in business quarters. In some places they were so narrow that the chairs would scrape both sides at once. Dried rats in great quantities hung up in the food shops for sale.

William's love for yachting and boating generally made him especially interested in the river population of Canton. He was accustomed to the narrow quarters of their own boat, the *Tsat-sawassa*, but never had he imagined that people could be born and married, live and die, rear their families and marry off their children without ever having a home on shore. There were some 350,000 boat-people in Canton at the time of William's visit. They lived in small *sampans* that lined the river banks about ten deep and simply choked all the small canals. A boat perhaps twenty feet long would hold a family of six or seven. Chickens hung out over the stern in a basket, which served as the chicken yard. Some of the children and women tied empty cans to their backs to act as a life preserver if they should fall overboard. A Chinese would seldom rescue another because the rescuer has to keep the rescued for the rest of his life if he happened to want to be kept. At times they bargained with a drowning man before pulling him out.

The work of the Y.M.C.A. in Canton concerned William. One afternoon he entered into a conversation with a young businessman who professed to be a Christian and emphasized the point that he always went to church. The start of the argument was that he was upset over missions, claiming that they were no good. As William tried to defend them and as they headed deeper into discussion, he soon realized the man was an infidel, not believing in anything the Bible said. The man believed that as William became older he would change his way of thinking. Flustered, William chided himself for his lack of Bible knowledge.

In a Christmas letter to his family, William from his hospital bed wrote:

> This is my first Christmas away from home and my first one spent in bed. It is rather different from what I suppose is going on at home. But I am not kicking. As I lie here several thousand miles away, home seems pretty nice and I feel it would be fine to be there. But when I do get back, it will be nice to think that I've been out here. We may get home before the first of September by a good deal, but cannot tell just now.

His homesickness could not be disguised, but as he became stronger the desire to shorten their trip passed away. The trip to Java had to be canceled and their plans for India curtailed, but what he and Mr. Erdman lost in this way was more than made up by the deepening friendship between them. Of those days Mr. Erdman wrote:

> His Bible was always on his bed in the hospital, except when the fever was at its height. I remember finding him pouring over the tenth chapter of Genesis one morning, with

a new interest in its geographical and ethnological statements aroused by his first impressions of new races and men of other tongues. It was a little Bible with fine print, too fine indeed for practical use, but it must have become dear to him, for I have seen it since, open, on his study table at Princeton.

The voyage to India completely brought back his strength and he was eager for all possible excursions among the foothills of the Himalayas, at Darjeeling and elsewhere, and for opportunities not open to the ordinary tourist, of shooting the spiral-horned black-buck when we were visiting friends in an isolated mission-station in the Central Provinces. His interest in the archaeological and architectural features of the Orient was rapidly increasing, quickened by visits to the wonderful temples in south India and by the fascination of the Taj Mahal, and his imagination was stirred by the monuments of Egypt. In the closing months of travel, his growing interest in the achievements of man was manifested in what was to his fellow-traveller at least an unexpected appreciation of the art treasures of the galleries of Europe. But all the time, though one did not realize it then, he was being specially impressed with the spiritual destitution of the people of the countries we were visiting.

Sunrise over the Himalayas was the sight of a lifetime! William and his companion had been in India for two weeks. They had left Calcutta the night before and had come up from the teeming plains of the Ganges by a mountain railway with a gauge of only two feet, through a dense jungle which did not lose in interest because "everyone said it was full of tigers and leopards"—a regular Mowgli jungle! It was misty when they reached Darjeeling, cold enough to make them realize that they were at an altitude of seven thousand feet. Few Hindus were to be seen, but in the crowded bazaar they found themselves surrounded by hardy mountain people, distinctly Mongol in appearance. There were Tibetans clad in sheepskins, from the land of mystery beyond the Himalayas; Nepalese and Bhooties from the equally forbidden countries lying to the east and west, and even enterprising merchants from China.

It seemed a little strange, on leaving the railway, to have one's things carried up the steep hill-paths by *women,* and at the hotel to have *men* chambermaids as well as waiters. But

the women of Bhootan were said to be the strongest in the
world. Barefooted, with large triangular baskets on their backs
and the help of a strap that went over the head, they carried
the heaviest loads, apparently with ease. Men and children
shared the labor, carrying stone, wood, grain, or whatever necessary up the steep hillsides—sturdy, healthy, cheerful creatures, a contrast in almost every way to the enervated people
of the plains. But nowhere in Bhootan, Nepal, or Tibet was
there a voice raised to tell these mountain races sunk in im-
morality and living in fear of demons and death of the one and
only Savior.

The next morning was still misty, and they were not called
at 4 A.M. to take the expected ride to Tiger Hill. But about 6
they woke to their first view of the highest mountains in the
world. Standing on the hotel porch, they looked out across deep
ravines filled with mist at the mighty range of the Himalayas.
The ranges they could see from the hotel were about forty miles
away and consisted of about ten peaks of which Kinshinjunga,
28,000 feet tall, was the highest. They were a solid mass of
snow, towering above them and clearly outlined against the blue
sky.

Their first view was very good but they had a better one
the next morning. They got started a little after 4 A.M., while
the stars and moon were still bright, for Tiger Hill. This "hill,"
only nine thousand feet, was about 6 miles from the hotel.
William enjoyed the horseback ride very much although he was
extremely cold. They got to the top just as dawn began to break
and the effects of light and shade were wonderful. To their right
was a wall of snow-capped peaks about 20,000 feet high,
stretching away for 100 miles. Directly west was the great range
with Junga. Then more to the left was a line of foothills about
11,000–12,000 feet high, wooded and without snow. Beyond
these, when the sun got higher, the peak of Mt. Everest, a
hundred and twenty miles away could be seen. With field
glasses they could see distinctly the sharp lines and great bare
cliffs. It was an unforgettable experience for them.

By contrast to this beautiful, pure, and lovely scene, touching evidences of the unsatisfied longing of hearts that search in

vain for comfort amid life's mysteries were all around them at Darjeeling. The faith of the mountain people was more simple and appealing than the heathenism of the plains.

It was at Madura, near the sandy, southern point of the Indian peninsula, that they had their introduction to the worship of Siva, whose mark—a horizontal smear—they had seen on so many foreheads. Imagine "a hot plain, a red road, shaded by the foliage of great overhanging trees in which monkeys were playing; the village fold coming home from the fields in the evening time; the village wells surrounded by women and girls with their water-jars; bullocks and buffaloes resting after the toils of the day, and the smoke of little wood or weed fires filling the air." In such surroundings they spent the night at a bungalow before visiting the great temple at Madura, one of the largest of the Dravidian temples of southern India. Covering twelve acres, it dominated the surrounding country with its massive *gopura*, something between pagodas and pyramids, rising to a commanding height above each entrance. William's description of this place shows his reaction to Hinduism seen for the first time.

January 1905

The Madura temple has five large *gopura* which are over two hundred feet high and four smaller ones. The outside of these structures is a solid mass of carved stone images of Hindu gods. Inside the wall is another enclosure with its *gopura*, and inside this is the sacred place which none but Hindus are allowed to enter. The rest of the space is taken up with bazaars, priests' quarters, etc. . . . The interior of the temple contains many images and corridors with wonderful stone monoliths. In the center is the "Tank of the Golden Lilies." I am sure I didn't discover any appropriateness about the name. The water was covered with green slime, and yet pilgrims were washing themselves and their clothes in it as well as drinking from it. It is supposed to wash away their sins. . . . Of course we were not allowed to go into some of the inner chambers and I guess it was just as well, for the worship of Siva to which the temple is given over is the foulest thing imaginable.

The three principal Hindu gods are Brahma the creator, Vishnu the preserver and Siva the destroyer and reproducer. All the large temples we have seen and innumerable small shrines are dedicated to the worship of Siva. You probably know something about this already—but if you don't I can't tell you, as it is too awful. The fact that this vile teaching is the most universal and popular thing in Hinduism is enough to offset everything that Hinduism may have done for the people, if it has done anything but degrade them.

It makes me tired to have a person who knows little or nothing about it say that these people are as well off with their religion as we are with ours, or rather that theirs is as good as ours. Five minutes' explanation of facts in any one of a dozen temples I have visited would disillusion such a person.

He would not put in plainer language the things these temples stood for: the deification of lust, the actual worship of symbols of vice, and the slavery of tens of thousands of women and girls "married to the gods." Around the temples in this part of India many monkeys gathered and were looked upon as sacred. One who knows the conditions wrote, "Wealth and labor could not have been devoted to baser practices than the erection of the vast enclosures dedicated to Siva and Vishnu. Even the sacred monkeys are disgraced by association with indescribable vileness."

Another aspect of idolatry and superstition was seen when they reached Madras just in time for the annual festival of Juggernaut. The city itself was nothing to see. They arrived by carriage about 9:30 P.M. and drove toward the native quarter of the city. Groups of people hurried in the same direction, some on foot and some crowded into little bullock carts. The whole population seemed to be centering on one point.

Immediately entering the area there were crowds of people everywhere—men and women with red shawls about themselves, fakirs smeared from head to foot with ashes and dirt, naked children and nearly everyone with some kind of a caste mark on his or her face. The street along which the procession was to pass was dimly lit, adding to the strangeness of the scene.

Finally the approach of the car was heralded by the pushing of the crowds, a vanguard of men beating kettle drums, and a

number of men with torches. Then came a carriage, a truly
wonderful sight, drawn by two long lines of men. It was a
square shrine on wheels about thirty feet high. The whole thing
was a solid mass of gilt and was brilliantly lit up by torches.
The men raised a great shout and then pulled the clumsy affair
a short distance, stopped, then started again with a shout, and
so on. Since the British Government had come into power, the
practice of people throwing themselves beneath the wheels of
the carriage to procure an instant place in heaven had been
stopped. Nevertheless, one can easily see how a religiously
fanatical people could, under the excitement of the moment,
do such a thing.

Soon they arrived at Benares, the sacred city on the Ganges,
which was much the same as when Macaulay wrote, "It was
commonly believed that half a million human beings were
crowded into that labyrinth of lofty alleys, rich with shrines
and minarets, and balconies, to which the sacred apes clung by
hundreds. The traveler could scarcely make his way through
the crowd of holy beggars and holy cows. The broad and stately
steps which descended from these swarming haunts to the bathing places were worn every day by the feet of an innumerable
multitude of worshippers."

William was rather disappointed in Benares as a sacred city;
it was far too dirty and its temples were comparatively poor
and small. However, it had interesting features, of which the
ghats were foremost.

The ghats were steps or landing places that lead down to
the Ganges and lined almost the entire waterfront. Some, in
fact the majority, were bathing ghats for all classes of people.
There was only one burning ghat where all the dead of Benares
were cremated. The city is so holy for the Hindu that death
within its precincts practically insures eternal happiness. Therefore pilgrims went there simply to die. One afternoon William
and Mr. Erdman took one of the boats along the river, enabling
them to see the humanity continually bathing in the sacred
stream, washing themselves and their clothes in it, praying in
it, drinking from it, and throwing their dead into it. Down-

stream from this they could see people of all classes doing their
religious duties. The burning ghat was not a pleasant sight.
Several corpses were in the midst of cremation. Bodies were
placed on piles of wood in plain view and the ashes were thrown
into the Ganges, with people bathing not fifty feet off. All day
long, throughout the year, the smoke of one or more pyres rose
from this place. Another method of disposing of the dead which
they observed several times was to weight the bodies with
stones and drop them in midstream.

Holy men and priests die, if possible, looking out over the
river. As they passed down the river, they saw an old man, a
living skeleton, seated on the bottom step near the water with
a friend propping him up. When they came back he was dead.

The city itself was a dirty hole, full of beggars, fakirs and
temples, with narrow streets in which sacred cows, donkeys
and goats ran loose, getting in everyone's way. In the midst of
this Hindu sanctum was the Mosque of Aurungzebe, the Muslim invader. He built it in the center as an insult to the Hindus,
and his present followers entered by the side door because the
Hindus blocked up the main entrance.

The temples were located in a crowded part of the city. Of
this William wrote:

> The temples are disappointing . . . and are very dingy
> places indeed. We were only allowed to look in and not to
> enter, of which I was not sorry. Cows came and went with
> impunity in the Golden Temple, which was positively sick-
> ening even from the doorway. The "Well of Knowledge" was
> a foul-smelling hole into which everyone threw flowers and
> water. We didn't approach very close, though the priest
> wanted us to make an offering of flowers.

Here the millions came and went, still seeking to wash away
their sins. The sacred cow was still the symbol—more than the
symbol: the embodiment—of the Hindu's highest hope, and if
they could not die by the Ganges, even scholarly men would
send for a cow to be brought into their room and had the hairs
of its tail spread over their faces that they might breathe their

souls away in the most sacred atmosphere they knew.[1]

From Benares the travelers passed on up the Ganges to Allahabad, at the junction of the Ganges with the Jumna—another focus of idolatrous worship, even though at one time it was for centuries under the heel of Muslim power. They reached the city as the annual Mela was commencing, when thousands of pilgrims were pouring in from far and near. Allahabad was the site of "the greatest Mela in India, when more than a million devout Hindus poured up from all over the land to bathe in the mingling of the waters of the two sacred rivers. There was probably no religious spectacle equal to it anywhere else in the world. Under no other religion and in no other land could hundreds of naked men with matted locks and grotesquely daubed bodies have been regarded as the embodiment of holiness."[2]

It was these fakirs, by their devotion as well as the sadness and weariness of their faces, who especially interested William. All the questions he wanted to ask at Allahabad found ready answers, for they were privileged to have as their escort a missionary who had been long in India. "You can learn more from a missionary in half an hour," he wrote with appreciation, "than you can pick up yourself in a couple of months of travel."

Dr. Lucas had been a missionary in India for thirty-four years, traveling into the country and visiting villages during the week. He had been promised an elephant to use at the Mela, so Saturday William and Walter joined him on his journey to procure the animal. On the way, they passed groups of pilgrims, some in bullock carts, but most walking. Many of the men carried baskets in which Dr. Lucas explained they would carry bottles of the sacred water back to their friends far away after getting a priest to seal it and mark it as the original article. Groups of women passed along the road chanting mournfully.

---

[1]There were temples like the temple of Vithoba, at Pandharpur, the great place of pilgrimage in the Deccan, where the cow was actually made an object of worship. The belief that the excretions of the cow have power to cleanse men from sin was almost universal among Hindus. (*Report on India and Persia*, Dr. Robert E. Speer, 1922, p. 152.)

[2]Ibid., p. 54.

All the pilgrims had the same sad expression on their faces, no trace of hope or happiness. They had been coming there as their ancestors before them, and yet they were just as bad off as ever. Nevertheless they kept on coming.

After some delay the elephant appeared and they clung to its back while he got on his feet, somewhat in the fashion one would upon a camel. From the back of this creature they had a splendid view of the sea of turbaned heads. The road leading up to the levee was lined with shops containing all sorts of things. Bottles for holy water, powder for caste marks, flowers for offerings, jewelry, shawls, etc. This levee was a good place to watch the approach of the pilgrims. They would come up the slope until they saw the river, then they would prostrate themselves in the dust and hurry on. William noticed women were much more painstaking than the men who often did not stop at all. The three continued on their elephant through the throng to the river bank, where they saw the crowds bathing. It was cold and some of the poor beggars nearly froze in their wet clothes.

When they had gone as far as they could because of the crowd, William and Walter with Dr. Lucas got down and walked to see the shrines and fakirs. At the roadsides were crowds of beggars with various deformities. Dr. Lucas explained that they considered any deformity a mark of divine power and, consequently, a holy thing. There were so many of these that a poor pilgrim could hardly be expected to offer something to each one. But they would walk down the line with a bag of rice and drop a few grains for each one. In this way small heaps of rice and other food stuffs would collect in front of each beggar.

The fakirs were the most interesting of all. Dressed in a loin cloth, the fakir's body was tatooed with ash dust, remaining a dull grey color. His hair was long, hanging like pieces of half-inch rope from the sprinklings of ashes and water. There were about two dozen of these men sitting along the road, but not all of them were self-torturists. About ten were either sitting or lying on boards of spikes. "To be sure," William wrote, "the spikes were somewhat blunted, but it must have been very uncomfortable until they got hardened to it." One man was sitting in a swing with one leg on the ground and his hands above his head. His arms were very small and shrunken after he had held them up that way for seven years. At first the pain was frightful, but now he could not lower them and had little movement in his hands.

The British Government had prohibited the worst of their self-torturing practices by the time William saw the fakirs. But it is difficult for Westerners to understand the state of mind that produces such results. To see a man kneel or lie on his back in the blazing sun with his head completely buried in the ground for a whole day at a time would not impress us with his holiness or with any desire to worship him. But it is very different with those whose only hope for the next life is the accumulation of merit in this one.[3] William wrote home, "No doubt a large number, of both sexes, choose a life of asceticism because they find it the simplest and easiest way of securing their daily bread. . . . But many of them show abundant evidence that they are sincere in their purpose, and persist through long lives of severe suffering and privation in faithfully following the course they have chosen."

At that very time there was in Bengal a woman who had been a fakir like those William Borden had seen at Allahabad. Having means of her own, she had visited all the most important temples in India to try to escape the burden of sin. She carried awful guilt over her husband's death at a young age, when she was only a child of thirteen. She attributed it to some wickedness on her part in a previous life. To atone for this unknown sin and to obtain relief for heart and conscience she spent seven long years traveling on foot from shrine to shrine, facing untold hardship and danger; but the burden grew only heavier as time went on.

---

[3] "The Hindu devotee," as Bishop Thoburn tells us, "flatters himself that he can by his penances of various kinds accumulate merit. The word *penance* to his mind conveys no idea of repentance, but solely that of a means of acquiring personal merit. In the next place he is possessed with the idea that matter is inherently evil, and that, since his union with a material body is the source of most of his misfortunes, he must make war on the body to liberate the soul. . . ."

She then determined to become a fakir. Deciding that she had not suffered enough, she gave three years to self-inflicted torture, honoring the formulas in the sacred books for pleasing the gods. She carried out her plan, though the sufferings she endured seemed incredible.

For one period of six months she sat without shelter in the sun all day with five fires burning around her, perspiration streaming from every pore. Even wealthy men brought wood and kept the fires burning as an act of merit. With no clothing but a loin-cloth, her body smeared with ashes, and her long hair dubbed with cow-dung, she was an object of veneration to the pilgrims, many of whom worshiped her as they fed the fires. At night she took her place in the temple, standing before the idol on one foot from midnight until daylight, her hands pressed together in the attitude of prayer, imploring the god to reveal himself to her.

Then, to increase her sufferings, when the cold season came with chilly nights, she went down at dark to the sacred pond and sat with the water up to her neck, counting her beads hour after hour till dawn appeared. And so she called upon Ram day and night with no response.

"If thou art God," she used to plead, "reveal thyself to me. Reach forth and take the offering I bring. Let me see, hear, or feel something by which I may know that I have pleased thee, and that my sin is pardoned"—but there was no sign, no rest, no peace.

When the years of her long struggles were finished, she went to Calcutta, cut off her once-beautiful hair, and threw it into the Ganges as an offering, exclaiming, "There—I have done and suffered all that can be required of mortal man, yet without avail!"

She lost faith in the idols and ceased to worship them.

"There is nothing in Hinduism," was the conclusion forced upon her, "or I would have found it."[4]

---

[4]For a more complete account of this woman, see the brief biography entitled *An Indian Priestess: The Life of Chundra Lela*, by Mrs. Ada Lee, Morgan and Scott, London, E.C.

This account was the brighter side of William's experiences in India and it was exciting to see and hear about the transformation that was slowly coming among the peoples of that great land.[5] It was evident that William was concerned for these things when he wrote his last letter from India. He wrote to his sister at Vassar College about the native state of Rajputana, of Jeypore, the capital, with its wide streets, pink houses, magnificent horses, trains of camels, and the "Barbaric splendor" of its Maharajah, who kept elephants and tigers to fight in his arena. On Sunday, however, William turned his thoughts on to other things:

> Rajputana Hotel
> February 26, 1905

Dear Mother,

I have just been reading over some of your letters and enjoying them so much. I do not expect to get any more until we reach Cairo.

Walt and I have Bible study together every day when possible, and I enjoy it very much. He is able to point out many things that are new to me, and I am beginning to see what a wonderful storehouse of good things the Bible is. I pray every day for all my dear family. I also pray that God will take my life into His hands and use it for the furtherance of His Kingdom as He sees best. I feel sure that He will answer my prayer. It strengthens me to know that you are also praying for this.

I have so much of everything in this life, and there are so many millions who have nothing and live in darkness! I don't think it is possible to realize it until one sees the East. I know it is no *easy* thing to serve the Lord, but others have been enabled to do so, and there is no reason why I should not. Mark 10:27.

---

[5] "It is the Christian's Bible that sooner or later will work out the regeneration of India."—The Maharajah of Travancore.

"It is a new heart that India requires, a transformation of life and character. Who can give that to India except a divine Savior? Send us missionaries who are not ashamed of the Gospel of Christ, who are not ashamed of the Cross; men and women who are living in close personal touch with the Master; men and women who have sat at His feet. They will meet India's need."—Words of an Indian Christian. See "Jesus Christ in the Thinking of Asia," *The Missionary Review of the World*, April 1924, p. 252ff.

Among the letters he had been re-reading was a sheet of paper he had carried with him all the way from Japan—not a letter, only a few verses in his mother's writing sent to him for the birthday he had spent so far from home. All through college and seminary years he kept it. It was among his special papers to the end of his life. It read:

Just as I am, Thine own to be,
Friend of the young, who lovest me,
To consecrate myself to Thee—
O Jesus Christ, I come.

In the glad morning of my day,
My life to give, my vows to pay,
With no reserve and no delay—
With all my heart, I come.

I would live ever in the light,
I would work ever for the right,
I would serve Thee with all my might—
Therefore to Thee I come.

Just as I am, young, strong and free,
To be the best that I can be
For truth and righteousness and Thee—
Lord of my life, I come.

5

COMMITMENT OF THE HEART

Summer 1905

Age 17

The meaning of being a Christian is that in response for the gift of a whole Christ I give my whole self to Him.

—Alexander MacLaren, D.D.

It was not until they were in Rome that William received a reply to his letter from Japan concerning his commitment to the mission field. His mother understood and rejoiced; his father wanted him to wait until he was twenty-one before committing himself to any vocation. In the meantime, the travelers had visited not only China, the Straits Settlements and India, but also Egypt, Palestine, Asia Minor, and the chief treasure cities of Greece and Italy.

They spent two weeks in Rome. The first afternoon they drove by the Colosseum, through the Arch of Constantine, around across the Tiber and back to their hotel, stopping at the Pantheon on the way. William found the Colosseum fascinating and the two spent quite some time going over it from top to bottom. Much of it had been excavated and the old pavement outside the amphitheater on the side opposite the Forum laid bare. A wooden model, a reconstruction of the original, gave one a very good idea of what it must have looked like in all its splendor.

The Pantheon was the only building of ancient Rome that was well-preserved. The very large dome had a hole, thirty feet across, in the center. The *caldarium* (hot room) of the baths was always made in this way, a dome with a hole closed by bronze doors in order to be able to control the temperature of the room. The Pantheon was at one point the caldarium of the baths of Agrippa, son-in-law of Augustus.

Dr. Forbes, lecturer and leading archeological authority who had been in Rome thirty-four years, accompanied William and Mr. Erdman three times around the city. They found him extremely interesting. He took them to the Patine Hill, the Forum, Tivoli, and Hadrian's Villa. His talks were stimulating and instructive, given as they were on the exact spots where the events related took place. They were shown where Cicero delivered his orations and the spot where Julius Caesar's body was burned.

Romulus and Remus, William learned, were facts and no longer legends. The legend of the wolf was explained by the fact that the wife of Faustulus was named Luca. (Faustulus was one of the Sabines who lived by the Tiber, and his wife brought up Romulus and Remus.) In the quarrel between Romulus and Remus, the two parties were led by Faustulus and Quintibius. The legend was that these two men were buried where they fell. Dr. Forbes had discovered their tombs seven feet below the level of the Roman Forum.

William enjoyed the collections of antiques and was impressed with the many statues of Rome.

Venice brought delightful relaxation with its watery streets and gondolas. After dinner they strolled over to St. Mark's to listen to a band. It was warm for June and they swam every day at the Lido followed by afternoon-tea, which was much appreciated after the sightseeing of the morning, while evening was spent in a gondola, meeting friends, listening to music, and watching the lights over the water. In the Doges' Palace they met an American party of seven young ladies with a chaperone who proved to be friendly as well as interesting. So the week in Venice passed all too quickly, filled with many interests. William recounted:

June 4, 1905

> Mrs. A. invited us to go out in their gondola last night. It was simply great! The lights on the Grand Canal and the little dark Rios were a picture. We went way up to the northeastern corner of the city, to the Three Bridges, and then out by the Guidecca and back down the Grand Canal. We lay alongside one of the singing barges and listened to the music for an hour or so. It was fine! I suppose you know all about it, for you and father must have enjoyed just such nights here together. I think I would like to come here on my wedding trip, if I ever have one. . . . Walt and I were remarking the other day that we had only met three American girls on our whole trip, until now. There's nothing like a real true American girl: French, German, English or Irish aren't in it!

In the midst of all this pleasure, however, William earnestly thought of deeper things. His desire to be a missionary never wavered. The thought of this never left him and he looked forward to missionary service with anticipation. He planned therefore, over the period of the next four or five years, to prepare himself for his future. Mr. Speer's book *Missionary Principles and Practice* looked at missionary work in the light of educational, medical, and evangelistic needs and related them to different countries. William found this a great help. He decided that he did not want to go through a seminary, but felt a thorough study of the Bible was what he needed. Agreeing with Dr. Torrey, William declared, "It's much more important and profitable to know what God has to say on a subject than what men have to say." He desired some medical skills, enough to raise him above being absolutely helpless and ignorant; but he did not want to try to form plans of his own without letting God do things for him, for then he knew it would be right.

In a letter to his parents he mentioned his completion of Mr. Speer's book.

> It has helped me a great deal. . . . He shows very clearly what the motto, "The Evangelization of the World in this

Generation" means, and how perfectly possible it is, provided we pray the Lord of the harvest to send forth laborers.

There was something inspiring in this for William, something worth every effort to accomplish. On his knees William prayed earnestly for mission work and for God's plan for his life and for the lives of everyone of his family. With college so near and so many opportunities at hand he knew he needed God's direction in everything, small and great.

A month of their trip had been saved for England; but before crossing the Channel, a brief visit to Switzerland introduced William to real mountain climbing, which was to become his highest enthusiasm as far as personal enjoyment was concerned. Their first mountain was the Titlis, 11,000 feet high, and with nails in their boots and a good guide they set out from Engelberg.

They walked that afternoon for an hour and a half to Trubsee, where they found a little hotel perched on the edge of a cliff overlooking the town and valley of Engelberg. It was wonderful, and after their walk they found a simple Swiss meal refreshing. There they drank their first glass of fresh milk since leaving America. Behind the hotel rose the range of snowy mountains, some of them quite peaked. The Titlis summit was entirely covered with snow.

At 2:15 A.M. they rose, and after eating they joined two other parties. Slowly but steadily, hardly stopping at all for an hour and a half, they covered a sloping foothill and crossed snowfields before stopping for a moment's rest.

From there on it was all snow and quite a struggle, but they reached the top in about an hour and twenty minutes. It was about six and the sun was up, giving considerable warmth. The view of the mountains over toward Interlochen, Monte Rosa, and the dome in the distance was worth the three hours of hard work. William felt great; the last stretch had gone very easily as he had gotten his stride and second wind. After they had eaten a little they started down, Walt leading and the guide following. They slid wherever they could, standing up and leaning back on their alpenstocks. It was great sport and they laughed and shouted all the way down. After a while the thin-

ning crust made it impossible, so they would break through the
snow and tumble over. After stopping a few moments at the
hotel to gather their belongings, they continued down to Engelberg, getting the 9 A.M. train back to Lucerne.

In some ways the best was reserved for the last, for the
travelers reached England in the midst of London's prime season, when the international championships were being contested in tennis, cricket, and other sports. Paris had been delightful, and Borden had taken special lessons in a school for
chauffeurs, learning to drive a car in the Bois de Boulogne. He
had wandered past miles of paintings in the Louvre and had
marveled at the glory of Versailles. But the Anglo-Saxon blood
in him rejoiced to set foot on British soil. "What Bliss to be
back in a land," he wrote, "where people talk English!"

The tennis matches at Wimbledon were exciting and on
Wednesday they went to the Henley Regatta at Henley on
Thames. They rented a canoe and paddled around among the
crowd. In the very first boat they passed, William spotted his
cousin Barbara and her friends. It was remarkable finding them,
considering that there were ten thousand people there. They
stayed for the morning races and returned to London about
two, after witnessing the American eight defeated by the famous Leander crew.

They visited St. Paul's Cathedral one day and climbed up
to the whispering gallery and down into the crypt to the tombs
of Wellington, Nelson, and other notables. The Band of England and Exchange are in that part of town, so they visited them
as well. On the way back they went down a little court off
Fleet Street and saw the Church of the Knight Templars, a little
old quaint building. Oliver Goldsmith's Tomb was just outside.
William felt the most interesting thing they did was to lunch at
the Cheshire Cheese. This was the original Inn at which Dr.
Sam Johnson and others used to meet, "Ye Olde Cheshyre
Cheese."

In the afternoon they went over to Lord's cricket grounds
to see the Cambridge-Oxford match. Evidently it was quite a
social event, as everyone there was dressed in their finest.

There were museums and art galleries to see, the House of

Parliament, Westminster Abbey, and Hampton Court. There was boating on the Thames, shopping, calling on friends, and more than one visit to Shepherd's Bush where "the finest tennis in the world" was being played. And amidst it all there was a new and deeper gladness, for William had come to perhaps the most vital experience of his life. *"I believe and I belong"* was now to have new meaning, as he wrote to his mother:

> Hotel Russell, London
> Friday, July 7, 1905

Dear Mother,

I thought I would write you two letters this time, as I have several things to speak about. Last Sunday and Monday were a sort of convention to me. I went to four meetings, every one of which was fine.

Sunday morning, Walt and I went over to Dr. Campbell Morgan's church, to hear Dr. Dixon of Boston preach. The sermon was very good. As I took notes, I can tell you all about it. One thing he said after the Scripture reading was, "Don't test the Bible by the book. . . ." He is a man who preaches the Gospel, like Dr. Torrey.

Dr. Torrey, as you know, has been holding meetings here in London for five months. This last month or so he has been in a specially constructed hall on the Strand, seating about five thousand. Sunday was the last day of these meetings. Walt and I went in the afternoon. The hall was by no means full, but there were fifteen hundred I guess.

Dr. Torrey spoke about being "born again," and mentioned some of the foolish ideas people have about it. His sermon was meant to straighten things out. I know that my own ideas were somewhat hazy, and I wasn't at all sure about it. But I am now. The text was John 3:6, "That which is born of the flesh is flesh, and that which is born of the Spirit is spirit." Dr. Torrey gave five proofs by which we can tell whether we are "born again," born of the Spirit, or not. Every proof was a verse of Scripture. That's what I like, lots of the Word of God and little of man. The five proofs were very convincing and plain.

In the letter he only states the points, but in his notes he had gone into more detail. The proofs, as he wrote them, were the following:

1. 1 John 2:29. *"Every one that doeth righteousness is born of Him."* Righteousness equals such actions as are straight. Straight action is conduct that is conformed to a straight edge. And the straight edge of life is the Word of God. Righteousness equals the practice of such actions as are conformed to the Word of God. Do we practice righteousness? If we do, we are born of God.

2. 1 John 3:9. *"Whosoever is born of God doth not commit sin."* Sin is something done, a breaking of the law; and the law is the revealed will of God. Sin, therefore, is transgression of the will of God. *"Whosoever committeth sin transgresseth also the law: for sin is the transgression of the law."* 1 John 3:4. The regenerate man does not willfully and intentionally sin.

3. 1 John 3:14. *"We know that we have passed from death unto life, because we love the brethren."* The brethren are all those who believe in the Lord Jesus Christ. Love for the brethren, positive and negative, is explained in verses 16–18. We ought to love to the extent of giving our lives—literally, if necessary—as God did for us. "Let us not love in word, neither with the tongue, but in deed and in truth," v. 18. Love for the brethren is a proof of rebirth.

4. 1 John 5:1. *"Whosoever believeth that Jesus is the Christ is born of God."* Christ equals the Anointed One of God. Belief equals absolute conviction. Whosoever is convinced absolutely that Jesus is the Anointed One of God is born of God.

5. 1 John 5:4. *"Whatsoever is born of God overcometh the world."* A regenerate person has that within him which overcomes the world.

Summary: One who is "born again" practices righteousness; is not committing sin; loves the brethren; believes that Jesus is the Christ; and overcomes the world. We cannot do all this by ourselves, therefore what are we to do? Answer, John 1:12. "As many as received Him, to them gave He power to become the sons of God, even to them that believe on His Name." So we have only to believe in Jesus and receive Him, and immediately we have power to become sons of God.

(The next thing to do is to use this power. W.W.B.)

William hastened back to the evening meeting, even missing dinner at the hotel because of it. The hall seated 5,000 and

was filled to capacity, but a deep hush fell on the listeners as
Dr. Torrey gave his closing message. *Today verses Tomorrow*
was his theme, and men were made to feel that they simply
could not afford to put off the vital matter of salvation: "Today
if ye will hear his voice, harden not your hearts" (Heb. 3:7–
8).

"Boast not thyself of tomorrow, for thou knowest not what
a day may bring forth" (Prov. 27:1).

The wise man accepts Christ today; the foolish puts it off
till tomorrow.

Of his experience that night Borden continued in the letter
to his mother:

> After this Dr. Torrey called for decisions. Fifty or sixty
> came forward and confessed Christ. Dr. Torrey told us to
> speak to those about us. I had an awful tussle, and almost
> didn't, for I thought the people around me were all Christians.
> However I wasn't sure, and so decided not to be the foolish
> man of tomorrow. I spoke to a lady next to me and others,
> but they were all saved. However I felt much better, and know
> it will be easier to do next time.
>
> In the after meeting, Miss Davis sang the song "I Surren-
> der All" and an invitation was given to those who had never
> publicly surrendered, whether Christians or not, to do so then.
> I stood up with several others and we sang the chorus:
>
> I surrender all, I surrender all;
> All to Thee, my blessed Saviour,
> I surrender all.
>
> Dr. Torrey then gave us a little talk on The Way of Life.
> He also spoke on How to Keep on with the Christian Life
> When It Is Begun:
>
> 1. Look always at Jesus.
> 2. Keep confessing Jesus everywhere.
> 3. Keep studying God's Word, Matthew 4:4.
> 4. Keep praying every day, I Thessalonians 5:17.
> 5. Go to work.
>
> The first four I am doing and the fifth I will do.
>
> Well, when I got home that night I felt there was a dif-
> ference. You know the expression, "for heaven's sake," that
> I have used so much, I know it was wrong and yet I couldn't
> stop it. Before last Sunday I had been praying about it, but

not very earnestly I am afraid, for though I managed to keep
it from my lips, it got started several times. That night I prayed
not only that my life might be controlled but my thoughts
also, and I meant it. I expected a direct answer and got it the
next day, and I have been kept in that matter ever since. I
don't think I ever had any real definite experience like that
before, and it has strengthened my faith. And now I am praying more earnestly about things for which we have been praying some time. . . .

You won't be able to get any answer to me about all this,
but we will talk things over when I arrive.

A deep conviction that to accept Christ as Savior meant to
accept Him as Lord was part of this experience, and a conviction leading to action. Witnessing was the outcome. It was no
easier for William at seventeen to witness for Christ than it is
for other young fellows of his age. He was reserved by nature;
but he had taken a step that must have consequences. In his
journal he had written for that Sunday:

July 2, 1905

Fine address. I was greatly helped and surrendered all to
Jesus at the invitation.

Surrender in his case meant not only giving up worldly
amusements and indulgences, it meant taking on his Master's
yoke, living with Him for others, always and everywhere. And
it was very practical. The next Sunday he wrote to his mother:

In the evening I started out to call on E.W. at the Coburg
Hotel. I didn't feel just right about it, as I know you don't
like us to make such calls on Sunday. However, I went ahead.
Walking down Oxford Street, I came to a place where an
outdoor service was being held. Something told me to stop
and help, but I went on. I had almost gotten to the Coburg
when I heard the singing of another group. It was a Wesleyan
mission band holding a gospel service.

After the meeting was over, I spoke to a young fellow and
asked him if he believed in Jesus Christ. He said he didn't
and didn't ever intend to. We stood on the street corner and
talked until eleven P.M. He had evidently read some books
written by a destructive critic, and I wasn't well enough versed

to meet his questions in a way to convince him. He was a very nice young fellow, and gave me his address and said he would be very glad if I could convince him. I am going to get Pierson's *Many Infallible Proofs* and try some more with him.

And he did, spending an entire afternoon hunting the same young man up in Shoreditch, a very unattractive part of London. But the address proved to be fictitious. There was no such house or person to be found. It was a disappointment; but who shall say how great a blessing came to William—and to countless others—through his faithfulness in evangelism, which began with that full and glad surrender to Jesus Christ as Lord?

It is the surrendered life that counts, for through it, God can work.

PART II

YALE

The life that counts must toil and fight;
Must hate the wrong and love the right;
Must stand for truth, by day, by night—
This is the life that counts.

The life that counts must hopeful be;
In darkest night make melody;
Must wait the dawn on bended knee—
This is the life that counts.

The life that counts must aim to rise
Above the earth to sunlit skies;
Must fix its gaze on Paradise—
This is the life that counts.

The life that counts must helpful be;
The cares and needs of others see;
Must seek the slaves of sin to free—
This is the life that counts.

The life that counts is linked with God;
And turns not from the cross, the rod;
But walks with joy where Jesus trod—
This is the life that counts.

—A.W.S.

6

TRAINING THE MIND

1905–1906

Age 17–18

Wherewithal shall a young man cleanse his way? by taking heed thereto according to thy word. Psalm 119:9

Thy word have I hid in mine heart, that I might not sin against thee. Psalm 119:11

—William Borden's college mottos. The first he put up in his room at Yale, the second he wrote in full on the flyleaf of his pocket Testament.

It was at Camden that the reunion took place: the family's summer home on the coast of Maine which Mr. Borden had recently built. The golf, bathing, and yachting, delightful as they were, all took second place to the renewed family connections and especially the times when William could be alone with his mother. College was drawing near, and there was more to look forward to than to look back upon after the first few days.

William Borden plunged into college a month or so after his return to America. Yale with its fine old campus and still finer traditions was a new world to him, but one in which he was soon to take no unworthy part.

Upon his arrival in New Haven, John, his brother, came with him to 242 York Street. William's room was at the back of the house and had a large bay window in three sections with an immense window seat. His trunks had not yet arrived so William accompanied John to his suite: two bedrooms and a sitting room that he shared with his friend George. As they wandered around they met many other fellows busy unpacking and settling into their rooms. William's trunks arrived in the afternoon so he didn't get much unpacking done. That evening John took him and a friend to Mori's to eat. This historic little cafe was quite popular with the college men. The table tops hosted carved initials, and in one room there was a special table on which seniors could leave their trademarks.

After dinner William left for his room and about 8:30 a group of sophomores arrived and made him do a few foolish stunts. He sang them a song and attempted to "scramble" like an egg, a very difficult thing to do. After a few minutes Borden was left in peace for the rest of the evening.

The next morning he passed his Iliad examination and was now a member in full standing of the class of 1909. That afternoon he registered at Alumni Hall and was assigned to divisions and given study schedules. While watching the football practice he met Bob Noyes, a Hill fellow, who kindly invited him to dinner. That night he dined with him and some other fellows, after which they went over to the campus to see a wrestling match. Dinner had taken longer than usual so the match was well under way when they arrived. The seniors, without hats and with coats on inside out, were seated in a large circle with their torches on the ground in front of them. In the center were all the big "Y" men who were running the performance. Borden could only get a glimpse now and then of the doings inside, but the sophomores won the match by winning the third bout, the heavyweight match, after the first two had been draws.

After this, the whole crowd moved to York Street and for a few minutes things teemed with life. Borden and his friends, being more peacefully inclined, observed from his porch. Later, a drunken sophomore who had visited Borden's room the night before appeared and Bob Noyes firmly told him to leave Borden alone. After a few minutes, William left for John's to spend the night.

Friday morning arrived and Borden was on the field trying out for the freshman football team. With ninety-nine others trying out, he felt his chances were slim.

The opening of College brought out all sorts of opportunities for him. Nearly everyone was required to use a Greek or Latin translation in their studies. The majority smoked, went to the theater Saturday night, and did their studying on Sunday. There were some fine Christian men in the school and he hoped they would be able to do something, by the grace of God, to help the others find Christ. Borden began eating his meals next door with seven other men. Only one other fellow did not smoke or study on Sundays and he had hopes of becoming friends.

He knew he was in a position not to criticize others but to give a little of what he had received. Grateful to his parents and others who had influenced his life, Borden desired to share the teachings he had learned. Prayer was essential in his life. Walt told Borden in a letter that an old English lady in the mission had told him that she had prayed for them every day for the past year. Prayer had power! Borden recalled a little poem his parents had sent to him once, about the ploughman at his work, praying, and the missionaries wondering how their words had such power, "because they did not see someone unknown, perhaps, and far away, on bended knee."[1]

---

[1]The weary ones had rest, the sad had joy
That day, and wondered "how?"
A ploughman singing at his work had prayed,
"Lord, bless them now."

Away in foreign lands they wondered "how"
Their simple word had power.
At home, the "Gleaners," two or three, had met
To pray an hour.

Yes, we are always wondering "how?"
Because we do not see
Someone, unknown perhaps, and far away,
On bended knee.

President Hadley preached in Chapel that morning, and gave a good sermon for the opening of the college year. Only in impressing the necessity of having a fixed purpose in life and distinguishing between right and wrong. He neglected to say what their purpose should be and where they should get the ability to persevere and the strength to resist temptations, things which seemed rather essential to Borden.

A reception was held Friday night for the freshmen class to meet the president and the various teams as well as John Magee. A quartet added to the entertainment and refreshments were served. The informal gathering made it possible for Borden to meet many of his classmates.

Dwight Hadd and Henry Wright, son of the dean, were to have such a large part in Borden's experiences at Yale that it is important to understand their relation to the life of the university. From the published biography of Dr. Wright it is evident that he was in America very much what Henry Drummond had been in Scotland. His brilliant scholarship was almost lost sight of in his spiritual fervor, complete consecration, and passion for winning men to Christ. He had a genius for friendship, and was young enough (twenty-eight when Borden entered) to be closely in touch with student life. He had received his doctor's degree in classics and had already been on the faculty two years as a tutor in Greek and Latin. He had also been general secretary of the Yale Y.M.C.A. (1898–1901), and it was during that period of his post-graduate studies that he came to be a campus figure.

> Dignified, kindly, a trifle shy at times, always eager to be of use, he grew into the hearts of faculty and students alike. "In connection with my own undergraduate days," said Professor B.W. Kunkel of Lafayette College, "I look upon Henry's smile of greeting at the head of the stairs in Dwight Hall, as we came to the meetings, as one of the benedictions which helped me through the week."*

Dwight Hall, the home of the Y.M.C.A., was still, when

---

*From *The Life of Henry B. Wright*, by George Stewart, Jr. Association Press, New York, p. 32.

Borden entered Yale, what Henry Wright had made it. It stood for the high type of scholarship as well as Christian manhood. From the Sunday evening services, often gathering hundreds, to the group meetings and personal talks in the little room on the top floor, it was the scene of much of the best work done in the university. And it was the inheritor of a glorious past. For the Y.M.C.A., organized in 1881, had not been a beginning so much as a culmination of Christian activity in the university. It had been "adopted as the best channel for the expression of the rich heritage of two centuries of Yale's religious traditions."[2]

Founded as a college for training men for the ministry of the gospel in 1701, Yale had always had a deeply religious basis, and had been visited in the past by many remarkable revivals of spiritual life. Under the mighty preaching of Whitefield, then only twenty-five years of age, the first of these took place in 1740, and they had been repeated at intervals so that we read of a whole series of revivals under the presidency of the first Dr. Timothy Dwight, which continued through the lifetime of his devoted colleague, Professor Chauncy A. Goodrich. "As an undergraduate or instructor, the latter must have witnessed and was an important factor in all but two of the nineteen revivals that graciously visited Yale from the accession of President Dwight up to the Civil War."[3]

As far back as 1812–13, a revival which was distinctly a student movement had swept the college. Several members of the senior class had been praying, mostly unknown to each other, for a spiritual awakening. Active opposition was expected from one student in particular, Elias Cornelius, and definite prayer was made for his conversion. Not long after, a sudden and complete change in this man had made a great impression on the student body. He broke with evil companions and profanity, and soon was rejoicing in the consciousness of Christ's presence and power to save. "He led nearly twenty

---

[2]*Two Centuries of Christian Activity at Yale*, Henry B. Wright and others, 1901.
[3]Ibid. p.74

members of his own class to the Christian faith . . . and by his labors from eighty to a hundred of all classes were awakened to a new sense of their Christian responsibility."[4]

Another remarkable revival in 1825 was due to the prayers of a single individual of but little standing in the college. He invited members of the University Church of more influence than himself to his room and encouraged others to prayer and labor for the conversion of those around them. His earnestness was used of God, and a deeply spiritual movement was the result.

From the period of the Civil War to the visits of D.L. Moody, the control of the voluntary religious life of the university was passing more and more into the hands of the students themselves. Christian work by students for students in time became centered in the Y.M.C.A., under whose leadership several revivals of more recent date had taken place, including that of 1900, when John R. Mott and Robert E. Speer were so powerfully used of God that no fewer than a hundred undergraduates professed conversion.

Five years later, with a new generation of students, there was need for all the prayer and effort centered at the Y.M.C.A., into which Borden wholeheartedly entered. John Magee, now a missionary at Nanking, was the graduate secretary, and it was not long before he discerned the intense reality behind the young freshman's spiritual life and convictions.

"The school is not a knowledge shop so much as a great assay of human souls," wrote Professor Meigs of "The Hill." Borden was being tested at Yale in that great assay, and was conscious of the same process in the lives of others. All around him it was going on: men making or marring their future. To him the Word of God meant so much in meeting the temptations of daily life. He was finding such strength in the companionship of the Lord Jesus Christ that he longed to share these great realities with others. So the purpose was forming in his heart of attempting to start a group for Bible study among those who would not avail themselves of the influences of Y.M.C.A. Just

---

[4]Ibid. p. 68.

after chapel service that morning they had their class prayer meeting at which several of them spoke on the possibilities of the year. John Magee invited Borden to come to the Volunteer Band that afternoon. There were about ten present and they had a good meeting and a time of prayer and Borden was impressed with the Christian life some of the upper classmen lived.

Borden, having talked over the matter of his group Bible study class with a friend, decided that paraphrasing Galatians might be too deep for the sort of men to be reached. The object of these groups was to interest men who do not attend the Wednesday evening meeting in Dwight Hall with the Y.M.C.A. So he considered other methods of Bible study suggested by Dr. Torrey. He selected the book of John and began to prepare questions and answers for the study. He was excited because John was written that men might believe that Jesus is the Christ, the Son of God, "and that believing ye might have life through his name."

Those days for Borden were extremely busy. He had twelve recitations a week to prepare. Monday evening at 6:45, the Freshman Religious Committee would meet in the room of Bill Barnes, Vice-President of Dwight Hall.

Wednesday evening at 6:40, the 1909 Bible Class met in Dwight Hall, led by Dr. Wright.

Thursday evening at 6:45, Borden's Mission Study Class met. Herbert Malcolm, a member of the Volunteer Band, led the class.

Sunday started with Chapel at 10:30, then his class prayer meeting, which he helped lead at times. At 5:00 there was a meeting of the Volunteer Band and at 6:40 a general meeting was held in Dwight Hall. The preacher of the morning session usually addressed this group. Besides these things, Borden intended to go down at least twice a week to the Oak Street Boys' Club.

He was appointed chairman of a committee to promote interest and collect funds for the Yale Hall work in New Haven and the Yale Mission in China. Yet he still went out for football, which took more time than he wished it had.

It was at one of those many meetings in Dwight Hall that Borden met his friend, the one who more than any other was to share his college life. Of that first meeting and his own impressions, Charlie Campbell wrote:

> We were crowded together in Bill Barnes' room. Barnes was a junior at the time, Vice-President of the Y.M.C.A., and leader of the freshman religious work. Bill Borden was sitting on the floor with his back against the wall and his knees drawn up near his chin. I remember noticing him particularly. As we left the meeting he joined me and we walked back together to York Street. Bill told me then, as I remember, of his trip around the world and of his interest in missions. This was the beginning of the friendship which has meant so much to me.

> About the early days of our acquaintance I would like to say a little, as they show one of Bill's finest characteristics, real democracy. I lived my freshman year in Pierson Hall, the one college-owned dormitory on York Street and not considered so swell as the private-owned dormitories. I not only lived in Pierson, but away up on the fifth floor. Anyone had to have courage to climb to the top of Pierson. My first impulse after meeting Bill and seeing his room at Garland's was to hold aloof. I felt he was too well off, and imagined he would not care to have much to do with me. How appreciative I felt and how drawn to Bill when I found him climbing up those Pierson steps, not once but often! And what times we would have! There was always the religious bond that drew us together; but Bill's spirit of fun was sure to show itself, and a good "rough house" or game was in order. I think of one evening when we staged a complete track meet in my room and Bill was the heavy competitor in all the events possible.

> It was well on in the first term when Bill and I began to pray together in the morning before breakfast. I cannot say positively whose suggestion it was, but I feel sure it must have originated with Bill. We had been meeting only a short time when a third, Farrand Williams, joined us and soon after a fourth, James M. Howard. These meetings were held in Bill's room just before we went to breakfast. The time was spent in prayer after a brief reading of Scripture. Our object was to pray for the religious work of the class and college, and also for those of our friends we were seeking to bring to Christ. I remember so well the stimulus Bill gave us in those meetings.

His handling of Scripture was always helpful. From the very beginning of the years I knew him he would read to us from the Bible, show us something that God had promised and then proceed to claim the promise with assurance.

This group for prayer was the beginning of the daily groups that spread to everyone of the college classes. From the membership of two at the start, the group in our class grew until it had to be divided in sophomore year, and by the end of the year there were similar groups in each of the classes. It was not passed down from the seniors to the juniors, but came up from the freshmen to the seniors. And very real blessing was given in answer to our prayers—quite a number were converted. I remember one with whom Bill worked very hard, a fellow with a scientific turn of mind who wanted everything proved. Bill must have looked down with joy from the place to which he has gone when, some years later, this man came out brightly as a Christian.

Bill was always picking out the toughest proposition and going through thick and thin to win him for Christ. . . . His life, how true it rang! He came to college far ahead, spiritually, of any of us. He had already given his heart in full surrender to Christ—had really done it. He had formed his purpose to become a foreign missionary, and all through college and seminary that purpose never wavered. One can easily see the advantage this would give a man. His life was determined. We who were his classmates learned to lean on him and find in him a strength that was solid as a rock, just because of this settled purpose and consecration.

Unconsciously the young freshman was becoming a force in the best life of the university. To himself it seemed quite otherwise and he strove to overcome inconsistencies and weaknesses in his life. One Sunday Mr. Mott spoke on characteristics of leadership and that evening in Dwight Hall he shared strongly on sin, especially on "Be sure your sin will find you out." At the end of the service he asked those who wanted to learn how to deal with temptation to meet in another room. About three-fifths of the group responded, including Borden.

The following Sundays brought a different experience. A preacher with an international reputation led the services, but to an earnest mind grappling with the realities of life was left with much to be desired. To Borden the man was exhausting. His talks, smooth, subtle, and pleasing to everyone were interesting, but what he spoke of merely amounted to human ethics. As Borden said, "He takes texts simply as pegs to hang his own thoughts on."

Perhaps the preacher did not realize what that hour might mean as he faced the group in the college chapel. Had he had the vision of what lay behind in those hundreds of lives, the temptations and dangers, possibilities and needs, he surly would have wanted to give them more than just eloquence and ethics.

Even William Borden was having struggles. He was discouraged about his Bible class. It was very difficult to get started and there was so much to be done. Systematic Bible study of his own was at times inconsistent and he felt no encouragement from the preachers who came to campus. In his opinion, "we get the saddest bunch of preachers you could scrape up in the U.S.A., and today we had one from Scotland who almost takes the cake." William had a deep desire for a more satisfying and stable life.

The Christmas vacation was evidently a time when his armor was buckled on afresh and he came back to school determined to put first things first in a new way. He began to get up every morning in time to have Bible study and prayer before beginning the day's work. It made a vast difference in his life.

The term started well for Borden. Mr. Speer one morning read a part of Matthew 10:32-33, his subject was "Confession and Denial." Speaking on character as essential to strong manhood and religion as necessary to character, he challenged William. Speer went on to show that religion—Christianity—is a question of personal attitude toward Jesus Christ. It is confession or denial.

The Dwight Hall meeting was voluntary, but the room was packed with about five hundred. Some fellows were standing, a thing they wouldn't think of doing in chapel. Again Mr. Speer gave a powerful talk on "Apart from Me ye can do nothing," and "I can do all things through Christ which strengtheneth me."

One Sunday afternoon Borden began a study on the word *procrastination*. As a result he felt it was up to him to go and speak with a fellow student about attending Bible study. About 3:45 in the afternoon, he went up to his room and found him pouring over a magazine. William tried to start the subject but could not seem to get up the courage. He sat there for a solid hour scarcely saying a word and accomplished nothing. Since he had a mission band meeting at five, he asked his friend to accompany him, hoping to speak to him on the way to Dwight Hall. However William did not say a word.

Ned Harvey led the band meeting and gave the group a study from Philippians 1:6, 9–10. When he finished he asked if there was anything special to be brought up for prayer. William rose as he thought of the verse in James, "Confess your faults one to another and pray one for another." Hesitating for a moment and overcome with emotion, William read the verse and spoke about his experience. Knowing that to be able to be an effective evangelist elsewhere in the world, he would have to begin where he was at, William confided that he had failed to speak with a fellow that afternoon and wanted their prayers.

That evening William had another chance to talk with his friend. In a round about way, still cowardly and fearful, he asked if the young man would be interested in studying the Bible and the result was positive! After that Borden felt more confidence and faith that through Christ he could carry out what was begun. Philippians 1:6, "Being confident of this very thing, that He which hath begun a good work in you will perform it until the day of Jesus Christ."

Chapel that morning was filled with prom girls and, naturally, young men as well. Mr. Speer preached a message on distinctions between right and wrong. After the service, according to college custom, the sophomores lined up outside and made remarks about the girls as they came out. William felt this to be an unpleasant gesture. That afternoon at a fairly well-attended prayer meeting they discussed Sabbath observance. Various subjects such as studying, traveling, playing games, etc., were brought up. Finally one of the young men rose and reminded them of what Mr. Speer had just said—that if there was any doubt about a thing, it was pretty sure to be wrong and it was best to give it a wide margin. To Borden it seemed that just about "hit the nail on the head."

That William Borden was far from thinking himself better than other people comes out in many of his letters, but he was growing. In a letter to his parents he wrote:

> Today hasn't been just as I would have liked. The morning sermon . . . was simply "sad." However, our little prayer meeting was better attended and a better spirit shown in it than ever before. I went off walking in the afternoon. Tried to find Bethany Mission and as we failed, kept on walking and didn't get back until supper time. Spent the early part of the evening in watching one of the fellows do tricks, and now it's late and B. is studying. So you see I have been pretty successfully "hindered," or rather I have allowed myself to be, for I confess I didn't make much effort, sort of shirked my duty. Oh yes, and I absolutely forgot about our band meeting, and missed that. I don't know just what's wrong—but the fact is I've failed again. Guess I haven't fed upon God's Word enough, nor prayed enough. I *will* try again.

There was a group of men in college called the personal-worker's group, which met every Tuesday in Dr. Wright's room. James Howard, Charlie Campbell, and Borden were chosen from their class for the group. Dr. Wright said, "It doesn't mean any honor, it means work." There were about fourteen in the group. After Dr. Wright read a short passage and said a few words, there was a general discussion, each one bringing up his case, and then they prayed together. William found this an excellent way to get to know some of the best men in the college in an intimate way. Through this he began to realize more than ever before that a man's *true friends* are his Christian friends. This small gathering was a great help to him and accomplished great things at Yale.[5]

---

[5]Professor Benjamin Wisner Bacon, who was then college pastor, spoke of these gatherings as the very "heart of heart" of Christian activity at Yale. "They were held in the little room under the eaves on the top floor at Dwight Hall, none being asked save the little inside group whom Henry [Wright] and the rest believed to be 100-percent consecrated. You may be sure I felt it an honor to be with these heart-and-soul Christian boys. . . . Henry was of course always the leader, richest in experience, wisest in counsel, most indefatigable in effort. It was the very breath of life to him to be about his father's business."

Borden missed his devotions only once or twice that term. To him it was next in importance to accepting Christ. Realizing that when he didn't wait upon God in prayer and Bible study, things would go wrong. At a band meeting one afternoon it was brought out that "Except the Lord build the house, they labor in vain that build it" and "Apart from Me ye can do nothing." They all felt their need of God's help and the necessity for greater consecration on their part. William mentioned in a letter to his parents: "One of the fellows confessed that he wasn't wholly consecrated by any means, and I'm afraid I'm not. But I want to be. . . . Keep praying for me."

7

A HEART IGNITED

1906

Age 18

God has His best things for the few
Who dare to stand the test:
God has His second best for those
Who will not have His best.

I want in this short life of mine
As much as may be pressed
Of service true to God and men;
Help me to have Thy best.

—Selected

"If one would understand the student life of America at its best during the last three decades, he should turn to the student conferences," wrote the biographer of Dr. Henry Wright, "for there are focused the aspirations of Christian youth in its highest mood of dedication. . . . Among all the events of the college year making for emancipation of the spirit and dedication of life, he placed the student conferences first." In the middle and at the close of Borden's freshman year came two outstanding experiences of this sort.

The first was the missionary convention of the Student Volunteer Movement at Nashville, attended by over four thousand delegates. The Yale contingent was strong, and the way in which Charlie Campbell came to be included in it was a surprise to himself if not to his friend. The night before the delegation was to leave, Charlie was in bed and almost asleep when a number of upper-classmen filed into his room. William Borden was among them. They told him that it was financially possible for them to take one more delegate, and they wanted him to go. Of course he went, believing that Borden was behind it. It was the kind of thing, at any rate, that he was always doing in a very quiet manner.

What a time they had on that long train journey to Nashville! Borden and the others would adjourn to the baggage car occasionally, to let off steam in games that usually came from William's fertile imagination. One of his games went by the name of "hot-hand." (A game learned from watching sailors on a German steamer during his trip around the world.) The man who was "it" must face the side of the car with his eyes closed, supporting his head against the car. The rest would then group themselves behind him and anyone was at liberty to take a whack. After each impact he had to guess who it was that had hit him. If his guess was correct, the giver of the blow had to change places with him; if incorrect, another whack was in order. William loved this game. Then there would be high kicking contests and other games, all in the rapidly moving car.

They reached Nashville full of life and spirits and there they separated for the different homes in which they would be staying. Those days were wonderful and inspiring for all of them, especially Charlie, for it was there he gave his life to God in consecration for any work to which He might call him.

Among the speakers, secretaries of boards, and visitors to the convention, of whom there were hundreds, and the foreign missionaries representing twenty-six countries, one man stood out for Borden with a burning message. He was a man with a map, charged with facts and enthusiasm, grim with earnestness, and filled with a passion of love for Christ and the perishing. Samuel Zwemer made that great map live, voicing the silent appeal of the Muslim world. Two hundred million of our fellow creatures in the lands colored green on the map—two hundred million under the sway of Islam, held in a bondage more relentless and more deadening than any other on earth, and even more degrading to its women—what a challenge to the Christian church! From China to the west coast of Africa and from the steppes of Russia right down to Zanzibar stretched that great sweep of green, sparsely dotted here and there with centers from which Christian light was spreading. Yet, as Dr. Zwemer showed, never before had there been such open doors for the evangelization of the Muslim world. *"The hour is ripe,"* was the burden of his message, and he sustained it with startling facts.

Making full allowance for all that was being done by missionaries in Muslim lands, the speaker pointed out country after country, province after province still absolutely without the Light of Life as far as their Muslim population was concerned. Some had no missionaries at all, such as Afghanistan with its four million Muslims; some had missionaries among their heathen races but none for the followers of the prophet of Allah. In China, for example, with fifteen million Muslims, not a single missionary had been set apart for their evangelization. Yet the door was no longer closed to the inland provinces in which most of them were found. Dr. Zwemer urged:

> When the door opens we ought to press in, sacrificing our lives if need be for God, as the Muslims did at Khartoum for their prophet. If the call voiced by those who have already spoken moved us deeply, coming from Persia, from Turkey, from Egypt, from India, if that was a call from God, *what shall be said of the mute appeal of the seventy million of the wholly unevangelized Muslim world?* Shall we stand by and allow these seventy million to continue under the curse and in the snare of a false religion, with no knowledge of the saving love and power of Christ, not because they have proved fanatical and refused to listen, not because they have thrust us back, but because none of us had ever had the courage to go to those lands and win them to Jesus Christ?
>
> Of course it will cost life. It is not an expedition of ease nor a picnic excursion to which we are called . . . it is going to cost many a life, and not lives only, but prayers and tears

and blood. Leadership in this movement has always been a
leadership in suffering. There was Raymond Lull, the first
missionary to the Muslims, stoned to death in Algiers; Henry
Martyn, pioneering in Persia with the cry, "Let me burn out
for God." We who are missionaries to Muslims today call
upon you to follow with us in their train, to go to these waiting
lands and light the beacon of the love of Christ in all the
Muslim world. Did He not live, pray, suffer for Muslims as
well as for us? Shall we do less if the call comes? Let us be
like those Scots of Bruce who were ready to falter until that
man on the white charger took the heart of Bruce in its casket
and swinging it round cried out, "Oh, heart of Bruce, lead
on!" As he flung it toward the enemy and bore down upon
them you could not have held those soldiers back with bands
of steel. Say not it is the appeal of the Muslim world or of
the missionaries—it is the call of the Master. Let us answer
with the shout, "Oh, heart of Christ, lead on!" And we will
follow that cry and win the Muslim world for Him.

More Muslims in China than there are in Persia; more Muslims in China than in the whole of Egypt; more Muslims in
China even than in Arabia, home and cradle of Islam, and *no
one* giving himself to their evangelization—little wonder that
with a nature like Borden's the facts demanded a response.
"We do not plead for missions," Dr. Zwemer was accustomed
to saying. "We simply bring the facts before you and ask for
a verdict."

Borden went back from Nashville committed to that great
enterprise, should the Lord confirm the call. He did not say
much about it, but from that time his most intimate friends
knew that he was definitely considering work among Muslims
in some unoccupied field.

On the return of the Yale delegation, reports had to be given
in various meetings, and in a letter to his parents he wrote:

> Yesterday was a rather strenuous day and I'm glad it's
> over. Our prayer meeting was well attended and the fellows
> did very well. One fellow's testimony was especially good.
> He said he had gone down there (Nashville Student Volunteer
> Convention) believing that foreign missions were useless, but
> that he had come back ashamed of himself and thoroughly
> convinced that they were doing good. Another of the fellows

gave a brief sketch of the Student Volunteer Movement. Another told a little about Medical Missions. Harold Stokes spoke on The Inadequacy of the Non-Christian Religions. I followed, on The Adequacy of the Christian Religion, and told the story Dr. Leary of Malaita told us; also I made things personal and hope I hit somebody. Charlie Campbell spoke last on Responsibility, and did splendidly. I am indeed thankful for the way God helped us.

In the evening Ken Latourette, a senior, Charley and myself, spoke at the Calvary Baptist Church. I tried to say too much, and as I only had ten minutes, got balled-up and did rather poorly. However, the other fellows did very well, and as I came in between it didn't matter so much. I'm afraid there was a little pride and ambition inside. The three of us speak again Friday and Sunday evening next, and I'm going to be more careful.

At this time, life at the university came to a halt for Borden and his closest friends with the sudden death of one of their classmates. He was a very bright young man from Ohio who had come to the university with no reference for moral character. The faculty let him in hoping it would be a good influence for him, but it wasn't. He found the wrong crowd and pursued a wild lifestyle. On Monday he took ill and was taken to the infirmary, where it was found that he had pleurisy, pneumonia and water on the heart, the last being the most serious.

Borden for sometime planned to make contact with this fellow, but had never followed through. Few in the class knew his illness was serious until Wednesday, when rumor had it that he was dying. Charlie, Bill Williams, and Borden went to the infirmary to find that he was unconscious and not likely to live out the day. Immediately, they went back to Borden's room and prayed. About three that afternoon he died. It was a shocking reality for Borden to face knowing that the promptings he received prior were not heeded.

The class sent flowers for the funeral and wore mourning buttons for a month. Borden was selected as a chairman of the committee for the purpose of drawing up a letter of condolence to be sent to the family.

Desiring to help the other three wild friends of the fellow

who died, Borden went up to see them one night and found
them playing poker behind locked doors. And yet, it was not
hopeless. Charlie began working with a fellow whose lifestyle
was similar to the others. Formerly he avoided Charlie, but
lately had begun to seek him out as change took place in his
life. Many in the personal workers' group and the Student Volunteer Band prayed daily for this man and others at Yale who
had a deep need for Christ in their lives.

The flow of Borden's thoughts was changed a few days
later by an unexpected visit from his parents. It was early in
April, and everything was budding with the new life of spring.
To John and William it was a special pleasure to show their
father the college campus, and the joy of those hours was un-
shadowed by any premonition of coming sorrow. Strange to
say, it was only a week later that William was writing from
Chicago, telling of the grief over his father's death to his friend
Dr. Henry W. Frost of the China Inland Mission.

Friday, April 13, 1906

Father and Mother were east about a week ago and had a
fine visit with us. First they went to Vassar and heard the
debate, in which Mary did very well. This pleased Father
immensely. Then they came on to Yale, and John and I had
a nice visit with them. It was the first time Father had visited
either John or myself at school or college. After leaving us
they went down to New York, got Mary and went to Lake-
wood. There Mary spent a day or two with them and had a
fine time. . . .

Back in Chicago, Father was perfectly well apparently,
and had nice visits with most of his near relatives and friends.
Saturday evening last he was taken sick, and on Sunday became critically ill. It was then we were summoned. Mary got
here Monday evening in time to see him, though he was unconscious. John and I arrived on Tuesday morning, three or
four hours after he had passed away.

William was only eighteen, but from that time he took more
than a son's place at his mother's side. With him, love was a
matter of deeds rather than of words, and in the midst of his
college work he made time to write to her daily, with few

exceptions. What that correspondence meant, keeping him in touch with all that concerned her, bringing the strong comfort of his sympathy into her aching loneliness, only a mother's heart can understand. If it cost some sacrifice, some moments of weariness after the strenuous day, the letters never showed it. They were always cheery and tender, and frequently contained charges not to reply unless she felt equal to writing. He often went into detail concerning his studies, conversations with friends he desired to encourage, athletics, and prayer requests.

Borden's freshman year came to a wonderful climax at the Yale Summer Conference that followed commencement. Prevented from attending the student conference at Northfield on account of its early date that year, they arranged for a gathering of their own under the leadership of Dr. Henry Wright, availing themselves of the grounds and buildings of the Hotchkiss School at Lakeville, Connecticut. One feature of the conference was a special course of training given to men who were to be leaders of voluntary groups for Bible study in the following year, for Borden's plan of small separate groups was to be extended to all the classes. A canvass had already been made, and out of Borden's class alone more than a hundred and fifty men were reported as willing to take up regular study in this way. This meant the preparation of a large body of leaders who were eager to get all they could from the full program of the conference.

Half the substantial reporter's notebook Borden had had with him in London was filled with notes from this Lakeville Conference, showing how very much it meant to him. Even in those full days of meetings, sports, and teaching—he was leading one of the daily groups for Bible study—he found time to write with the same loving thoughtfulness to his mother.

Monday our regular Bible study groups started. The subject was Jesus and the Father. Beginnings are all hard, and possibly this was a hard subject to draw the fellows out on. . . . Today the subject was Jesus and Sin, a splendid one indeed, and we all got along much better. In my group is a Chinese nobleman's son. I'm not sure but that he is a Viceroy's son. He is one of our classmates, and is interested, as is shown by the fact that he is here.

In the course of study on student summer missions, Henry (Dr. Wright) is outlining for us ten studies on Traits of Manhood. We had *Honesty* this morning, and it was splendid. I must get some boys together as soon as I get back to Camden.

In his notebook Borden had written after one Sunday's talk:

Say "No" to self, "Yes" to Jesus every time. A steep road—hard work? But every man on this road has One who walks with him in lock-step. His presence overtops everything that has been cut out. . . .

In every man's heart there is a throne and a cross. If Christ is on the throne, self is on the cross; and if self, even a little bit, is on the throne, Jesus is on the cross in that man's heart. . . . If Jesus is on the throne, you will go where He wants you to go. Jesus on the throne glorifies any work or spot. . . .

If you are thirsty, and he is enthroned, *drink*. Drinking, the simplest act there is, means taking. "He that believeth on Me, out of him shall flow rivers of living water. This spake He of the Spirit." To "believe" is *to know*, because of His word. How shall I know that I have power to meet temptation, to witness for Him? Believe His word: it will come.

Lord Jesus, I take hands off, as far as my life is concerned. I put Thee on the throne in my heart. Change, cleanse, use me as Thou shalt choose. I take the full power of Thy Holy Spirit. I thank Thee.

I may never know a tithe of the result until Morning.

8

FRUITFUL WORK

1906–1907

Age 18–19

His lamps are we,
To shine where He shall say:
And lamps are not for sunny rooms
Nor for the light of the day;
But for dark places of the earth
Where shame and wrong and crime have birth;
Or for the murky twilight grey
Where wandering sheep have gone astray,
Or where the lamp of faith burns dim
And souls are groping after Him.

—A. J. Flint

It was the result of the step taken at the Lakeville Conference that sophomore year that Borden was drawn into most unexpected and fruitful work for others. The Living Water was flowing out in new, unlooked-for channels.

There were a number of questions that William Borden considered this year, but the one that he had to face first was a fraternity. There were five junior societies as well as three senior fraternities at Yale. Unless a man had been elected in his sophomore year to membership in one of the five, the senior societies would pass him by. Each of the upper-class societies received thirty new members annually and great secrecy was observed in all their proceedings. A fraternity man would "keep still" if his society were even mentioned. It was this secrecy and the exclusiveness of the system that troubled Borden, whose uncle had been one of the founders of Wolf's Head, of which his brother was a member. "He could have had anything here that he wanted," wrote Dr. Kenneth Latourette in this connection. But, though feeling no less than others how hard it would be to be shut out, Borden had his misgivings.

Shortly before the school year began, William asked his friend Charles Campbell to come to Poughkeepsie[1] to talk over the society question. He invited James M. Howard and E.F. Jefferson as well. Together they discussed questions such as whether they as Christians could belong to a secret society. Would such action harm or help their work for Christ? It was a new thought to most of them since they had taken the society system for granted and had never questioned whether it was right or wrong for them to join one of the fraternities. William, however, took nothing for granted. A servant of Jesus, he believed everything must be tested and bear Christ's approval before he would enter into it.

The element of secrecy was one of William's difficulties with regard to joining a fraternity. As a Christian he felt that he should not go into anything that he did not clearly understand beforehand. He also feared that the fraternity system led to the forming of cliques in the college. He did not wish to be set apart from his class. Furthermore, he did not wish to have anything come between him and God. He had given himself wholeheartedly to Christ, to be His follower pure and simple, and he wanted that relation kept always true. Therefore he felt he had no right to vow allegiance to any secret, man-made organization.

This attitude was entirely comprehensible to any thoughtful

---

[1]A place on one of the most beautiful reaches of the Hudson River, where Mrs. Borden had rented a house to be near Vassar College in her daughter's senior year.

Yale man who thinks back to his freshman year and remembers how certain men "lose their heads" and set about to make a fraternity as the be-all and end-all of existence. One classmate of Borden's said that he should consider his college course a failure unless he made Delta Kappa Epsilon among the first ten elected. Happily, such insanity does not continue long after the verdant stage. This man never made Delta Kappa at all, but joined another fraternity after its second election in his senior year, but did not think his college course a failure.

The discussions at Poughkeepsie brought out much that was to be said on both sides, but the men reached no definite decision. The first fraternity elections would not be until a month after college reopened, so Borden and his friends went back with the question more or less unsettled.

The position this small group held in the estimation of their classmates was seen in an interesting light. A short time before the fraternity elections were held, the class elected the "deacons." At that time, each class chose four men at the beginning of their sophomore year who acted as deacons in the University Church and were charged with responsibility for the religious work of their class. The day of the elections, William Borden, James Howard, E.F. Jefferson, and Charlie Campbell prayed that God would guide the choice so that the right people would be appointed. As it turned out, the four of them were chosen.

Soon after came the first elections to the junior fraternities. The four had talked together many times since their visit at Poughkeepsie and had discussed the society question from every point of view. Borden discussed the matter with Henry Wright, his mother, and a few others. The final outcome was Borden's decision to go into no society. The others decided to join if they had the opportunity.[2] William adhered to this decision all through his college course, never joining a secret society, though he did join the Elihu Club, a non-secret organization, at the close of his junior year.

That decision cost him a good deal, evidenced by letters he wrote to his mother:

---

[2] All three were among the first elected.

October 3, 1906

Last night I had several callers—two bunches of Psi U men, one of Delta K.E., one of Zeta Psi. But as I'm not worrying, it didn't bother me, and I was able to study between their visits. I knew most of them.

October 6, 1906

I have had more ups and downs in the last day or two than I've ever had before, I think. Nothing very serious to be sure, but annoying. Just at the present I'm recovering from a down. Your little notes are a great source of comfort and enjoyment. I am going out to get some exercise now, throwing the hammer.

October 18, 1906

Well, I guess I wanted to go in a good deal more than I realized. . . . I have not slept much the last few nights I know. The question yesterday resolved itself into this: Are secret societies a good thing—from the Christian standpoint, of course? I cannot feel that they are either good or necessary, therefore I cannot go into one and lend them my support. I hope that God will bless Jim and Jeff and Charlie and use them mightily, but I cannot see my way clear. It is settled.

He felt like a different man, he wrote as soon as this decision was reached. "Busy and happy" was his next report. The sacrifice had been great, greater perhaps than anyone realized, but the reward was great too. Far from losing influence by not being a member of a fraternity, Dr. Kenneth Latourette stated that "as a matter of fact, he had more influence with his classmates in his senior year than ever before." And this meant much, as is proved in connection with unexpected developments.

It was on his nineteenth birthday, the first of November, that John Magee, the graduate secretary of the Y.M.C.A., stopped him in Dwight Hall and asked for a few minutes' conversation. There were matters in which he needed help that he felt Borden could give.

New Haven, a seaport town midway between New York

and Boston, was a place where vagrants of all sorts were apt to congregate. Work was to be had on the docks, and it was a half-way house for tramps and hobos moving from one city to the other. It was also the location of the county jail, from which prisoners were constantly being discharged with no one to give them a helping hand; for while drinking saloons and infamous resorts were to be found in abundance, there was no rescue mission with its doors always open to those who needed succour. This state of things appealed to John Magee from a double point of view. He saw the need of the down-and-out; he saw also the possible influence of such a mission upon the college community as a witness to the living, saving power of Christ. And he believed that Borden would see and feel it too.

"For," as a modern writer has well stated, "there is an empiricism of religion which is worth attention. It challenges the skeptic to explain both the conversion of the sinner and the beauty of the saint. If religion can change a man's whole character in the twinkling of an eye, if it can give a beauty of holiness to human nature such as is felt by all men to be the highest expression of man's spirit, truly it is a science of life which works and one which its critics must explain. . . . Let the skeptic bring his indictment against the lives of those who attribute to Christ alone the daily miracle of their gladness."

What could the unbeliever decide, for example, of a man who had been the terror of the worst ward in New York, the thief who would not have hesitated, as he said himself, "to cut a man's throat for a five-dollar bill and kick him overboard, who was sentenced to fifteen years' hard labor in prison when he was only nineteen and came out only to sink ever deeper into drunkenness and sin with no power to break his chains—until Christ met and transformed him? Yet that man, Jerry McAuley, established in his old haunts the first of such rescue missions and was a means of temporal and spiritual blessing to thousands.

What would the skeptic do with the educated, able man of business, who became entangled in the meshes of the drinking habit, sinking from depth to depth of misery, haunted by crimes he had committed—a hundred and twenty forgeries against one man alone—tormented with the horrors of delirium tremors until his friends, home and wife were all gone and there was nothing before him but the jail or suicide? He had chosen the latter, yet that man, Samuel H. Hadley, became McAuley's successor in the Water Street Mission, and like him, an apostle of the lost. Truly "if any man be in Christ Jesus he is a new creation."

Knowing such facts as these it was little wonder that Magee and Borden began to pray that a similar mission be established, for the sake of the university no less than for the unfortunate. To his mother Borden wrote:

November 1, 1906

John Magee is trying his best to do just what we have wanted done—to develop the evangelistic element and spirit here at Yale. As you may know, Dr. J.W. Dawson[3] is to be here for a week in February. The present head of the McAuley Mission in New York is a college graduate who went down, down, and was converted about two years ago, Edward C. Mercer. They had him at Princeton recently, and John has been inquiring to see how it went down there. He found that it was fine, and he is going to invite him here to speak at Dwight. That's just what I've been hoping for, and I think you have too. John is really a corker and is doing a lot.

He had me up in his room today to speak about the need for a good City Mission here in New Haven. . . . The plan is to get a suitable building in the downtown district and have a real Rescue Mission, run by a man from Water Street, or some such place, and a few picked men from the University. . . . It would be great!—just the thing to take a few skeptics down and let them see the Spirit of God really at work regenerating men.

November 8, 1906

Last night I went over and saw Magee. Mr. Skinner and old Brother Martin (converted drunkards) met with us, and we talked over plans for the City Mission. I tell you it was inspiring to hear those men talk! . . . We decided to pray over the matter for a week and see what would develop. I hope to

---

[3] A well-known writer and preacher who had had remarkable experiences in revival and midnight meetings.

go to the prison with them a week from Sunday. They go once a month. The prospects for the Mission are very bright, and I feel sure we shall have it, if it is the Lord's will.

Meanwhile his classroom work was not neglected. At the close of his freshman year Borden had discovered that his marks were not up to Phi Beta Kappa standard, and he decided to change his habits of study. Previously he had gone on the method of studying up for each recitation just before it came. Now he set himself to prepare a day ahead, and never retired for the night without having all his preparation completed for the following day.

"It was a hard method to live up to," commented his friend Campbell, "and showed his strength of will. Think of what it meant on Saturday to get all Monday's work out of hand, for Bill never studied on Sunday. He would work until eleven or eleven-thirty at night, but not later. Then he could sleep quietly and be ready for whatever calls upon his time might come. It meant much in his mental make-up and when it came to examinations."

"I figured up yesterday where my time went per week," Borden wrote early in sophomore year, "and found that about thirty-five hours are wasted somehow. I am going to see if I can't systematize, so as to get the most use out of them."

The success in this endeavor was evident from the amount of work he was able to accomplish. His daily prayer-groups were still going strong during this time and he improved his marks in studies.

The responsibilities of class deacon were taken seriously by the four friends. It seems that the office, which was much respected, dated back to the founding of The Church of Christ in Yale in 1756. Up to that time the students and faculty had attended the old Congregational Church on The Gree, but it was felt that a different style of preaching was more suitable than what was given for the usual mixed assembly. Much opposition had to be overcome, but ultimately the University Church was organized along the Congregational lines. Therefore the officers were not elders but deacons; and the term "class deacon" was adopted to designate the students chosen by the undergraduate body as their representatives in church affairs.

In Borden's time the deacons held their meetings weekly, a committee of twelve men, four from each of the sophomore, junior, and senior classes, charged with the spiritual interests of their fellow students.[4] These meetings were times of sincere prayer for help and guidance and resulted in "strong friendships that gave a certain sense of unity to the religious life in the college." Borden and his friends had already been on the Freshman Religious Committee and brought to this board the same earnest aggressive spirit.

Borden, Charlie, and Jeff met together and divided up the class (about three hundred men). The plan was for each deacon to have a quarter of the class as his parish and to *know* every man. They felt it would be well worth the effort, knowing that this would be time consuming.

Every Wednesday evening, the deacons met with Joe Twitchell, the college Y.M.C.A. secretary. He was an amusing man, but very frank and good-natured.

December 10, 1906

> Mother, you will be pleased to hear that my friend is getting on very well in every way (the classmate who formerly boasted that he had broken every commandment but one). He leads a Sunday School class and has a Phi Beta Kappa stand in his studies. Rather a contrast with last year!
>
> Had my first exam today, Physics. It was very hard.
>
> Have received six Christmas invitations. Guess I'm still in society!

January 20, 1907

> We have had a fine time today, and I feel like singing the Doxology. . . .
>
> You remember I told you that the first meeting of our Bible

---

[4] "The verdict of men most in touch with life on the campus is that the morals and tone of the undergraduates are unusually high and clean, and steadily improving. That such is the case is largely due to the presence year after year of this small, earnest body of men, elected by the classes, but connected with and under the control of the Church, to lead the Christian work and set and example of manly living." *Two Centuries of Christian Activity at Yale*, "The Class Deacons," S.H. Fisher, p. 208.

Class with the new teacher wasn't much good. Well, Wednesday we had an extra good prayer meeting at noon, and had faith. The result was we had a *fine* meeting that evening, though not many fellows were present. Charlie and I spoke to Mr. C. afterwards and said that we were behind him in prayer. He was very nice, and we feel confident for the future.

My Mission Study class went very well on Thursday.

I am thankful to say I have been doing a little more real work for Christ. I asked N.S. to go and hear Gipsy Smith, and he said he would if possible. I also wrote to M.T., following up our talk at Camden. D.W. was on my heart, and I wrote a pretty plain letter to him. This is about all my long-distance work.

With F. I haven't done much more, but the door is open. My work with S. is going well. After our Bible groups today I had the best talk with him I've ever had. He's nearly there I believe.

Charlie has a new group started today (Bible Study) among some seemingly impossible fellows. He is getting hold of perhaps the brightest man in the class, who is also one of the most dissipated. . . .

At Band Meeting a Mr. Smeet from China spoke to us. Filled with the Spirit, he gave a wonderful message which stirred Ken and me deeply, and we are going to work more for volunteers out of 1909. . . .

Here on my floor things are going badly. The fellows play cards a great deal—most of it is gambling, and on Sunday too.

Things were running smoothly for Borden. The four deacons met again to go over with the group leaders about a new project for canvassing their class. Charlie and Borden each took a hard bunch of fellows and, after a little prayer, went trusting in God. The way opened up wonderfully and they each started a new group.

At this very time, they were planning for the rescue work which early in the year took shape as The Yale Hope Mission. The visit of two speakers, Dr. Dawson and Mr. Mercer, could hardly have been more opportune, demonstrating the power of Christ and the need in men's lives for such a Savior.

Mr. Mercer's talks opened men's eyes to the evil of the

"social glass," which aided to ruin him while in the University of Virginia. The scientific department of the university, with over a thousand students, began to move under the conviction of the Holy Spirit as never before. Borden sensed the need for reapers and felt that any day in which work is not done for Christ was a wasted day.

It was a welcome development, therefore, when a few weeks later the rescue mission was opened, which provided new opportunities for the work he and others were learning to put first in their lives. Much hope and prayer lay behind the modest beginning. Charlie Campbell wrote:

> A room had been rented in a cheap hotel in just the right quarter—the room which has been used ever since for the meetings. It had hideous dark red paper in those days. Later on, Bill bought the entire building, and we now have downstairs dormitories and shower baths, and a place in which clothes can be fumigated, as well as a good, inexpensive lodging-house upstairs, known as the Hotel Martin.[5] For two dollars a week a man can have a room to himself, a little home.
>
> But we had no such helps in those early days and did the more ourselves in consequence. I can remember distinctly how we carted hymn-books in my suitcase down to the hall for that first meeting. The handle of the suitcase broke and we had to hoist it up on our shoulders and carry it through the streets! Bill was heart and soul in it all. It was great to see him in those meetings—so earnest in his presentation of the truth and in dealing with those who came forward for prayer. Afterwards, he would often take men around until he could find a place for them to sleep, and pay the lodging-house charge himself so as to avoid putting temptation in their way by giving them money.

It was the sixteenth of March when this beginning was made, and before the month was over Borden was writing to his mother of a man from Water Street who was coming to live on the premises and take charge of the growing work.

> Mr. Bernardt was a graduate of the University of Georgia and did postgraduate work at Vanderbilt. He rose to the po-

---

[5] After "Daddy Martin," greatly beloved.

sition of cashier in the big Southern Express Company. Then, through gambling, he got into debt. This led to stealing, first a little, then more, then a large sum and he was caught. Result—five years in a southern prison which he found to be "a literal hell." He went in a comparatively innocent boy and came out "a fiend." He could get nothing to do so he deliberately became a professional criminal and was before long an international character. One of his sentences was to "work in the mines under the lash for *three and a half years, never seeing daylight*"!

In all, he spent over twenty-two years in prison. After the last term he "lost his nerve" and determined to be a man. He travelled eight thousand miles in search of employment, without success. At last, stranded in New York, he was about to commit suicide. On his way to the river he heard singing from the Water Street Mission and turned in. Nothing happened that night or the next, but the third night the great change came. I cannot tell you all about it—but he is a Christian now and no mistake!

His present job is clerking in a cheap Bowery hotel, but he is always ready, Mr. Mercer says, to go anywhere and speak for Christ. His ambition is to get into rescue work and devote his whole time to it. This is the man we have asked to come and take the Yale Hope Mission. All he wants is a clean place to sleep, three meals a day, decent clothes and some money in his pocket to "help the other fellow." Sixty dollars a month he says is too much, in addition to board and lodging, so we are to give him fifty.

Bernhardt was no disappointment. Many a man on the Yale campus as well as on the streets in New Haven had reason to thank God for his coming.

"The Yale Hope Mission is booming at present beyond all expectation," Borden wrote at the end of the month. "Bernhardt began last Sunday and that evening eight men came forward, several of them in dead earnest. I was unable to go down last night, but Magee told me that seven more were seeking salvation. Bernhardt is fine, and is taking hold of the work wonderfully."

9

SUPERNATURALLY NATURAL

1907–1909

Age 19–21

It takes great strength to bring your life up square
With your accepted thought and hold it there:
It is so easy to drift back, to sink,
So hard to live abreast of what you think.

—C.P.S.

It was characteristic of Borden and friend Campbell that they did not room together either in junior or senior year. But they were on the same floor in White Hall and had what they valued most, the opportunity of being helpful to others. Malcolm B. Vilas of Cleveland was Borden's roommate, a boy of fine character who had taken a positive Christian stand at the Lakeville Conference at the close of the freshman year. The suite they occupied had a study and two bedrooms facing the Yale gymnasium and West Rock. Next door lived Campbell and Louis G. Audette, and across the hall were two other classmates, Sandford D. Stockton and Frank Assman. It was a good combination, made up of very different personalities.

Every now and then they would get rid of superfluous energy in a big rough-house. They would nag Borden until they had him roused and then around the room he would go like a tornado, crushing all opposition. It was a sight to see! He was a fellow of unusual physical strength and knew how to use it to his advantage. Charlie Campbell found that the best way to treat Borden when he went after him was to give right in. This seemed to mollify him, while resistance only spurred him on to greater efforts. They used to have many tussles together but he was altogether too strong for the average man and, with his knowledge of wrestling, was more than a match for any one of them. They would laugh at him because of his strength and call him a "brute."

The activities in the religious work went along much the same. There were the Bible groups, the mission study classes, the daily prayer groups, the Wednesday-evening Bible classes, the Volunteer Band meetings and the Yale Hope Mission, all of which occupied Borden's time. The last was especially absorbing for him that year as he also took one night a week at the mission conducting the service.

During Christmas vacation of his junior year, Borden went with his mother and Joyce to the Lake Placid Club in the Adirondacks. It was a beautiful winter with several feet of snow on the ground in the mountains. William and his mother with their wonderful hospitality decided to have a house-party. Invitations were sent to Isabel Corbiere, Mary Abbe, and three of Charlie Campbell's sisters, as well as Mac Vilas, Bill Roberts, Lou Audette, and Charlie. All but Mac were able to accept, and they arrived on New Year's Eve.

How crisp the mountain air was as they drove up in sleighs from the station and started in for a glorious party! They cast off all thought of work and settled down to healthy outdoor sports. Borden was in the thick of it. After his guests dressed up in their old, warm clothes they set out for the toboggan course. The snow was soft and all kinds of stunts were possible. They spent much of the time trying to go down the hill standing on the toboggans. Four or five of them would stand on one toboggan and attempted to balance all the way down the frosty slopes. One would always lose his balance and upset the rest, sending them tumbling head first into the snow.

Over on the road, coasting on the bobsled was possible,

and near the club was good skating. One brisk afternoon the small group trudged off in the deep snow and climbed a little mountain nearby. Every night they would return tired, healthy, and ready for dinner and a good night's sleep. William simply reveled in good fellowship and sport such as this, and it did one good to be with him. He was an ideal host and always saw to it that his guests had an enjoyable time.

"For whosoever hath, to him shall be given" was certainly true in Borden's case, for one upon another, even in his junior year, responsibilities came crowding upon him. The Student Missionary Union of colleges in the Connecticut Valley held its annual conference at New Haven that fall and Borden was chairman at all the meetings. Months of preparation lay behind the success of the gatherings and the full responsibility for speakers and arrangements was on his shoulders. Stephen W. Ryder, a classmate who helped him, reminisced:

> As a stenographer and typist, I often took his dictation of letters to his friends. I specially remember quite an extensive correspondence which devolved upon him as chairman of Connecticut Valley Student Missionary Conference. His apologies, his thoughtful explanations and general care to avoid misunderstandings, his desire to please, encourage and inspire others often impressed me. He sought no subterfuges or excuses, nor dealt in flattery to serve his ends. There was always frankness and sincerity in his letters.

John Magee, among others, was impressed with the organizing ability Borden showed in handling this undertaking:

> Bill was busy enough with all he was doing in college to take the time of any ordinary man. But he seemed to have little difficulty in running this conference, in spite of the large amount of work connected with it, of which I had had experience. It was held in New Haven that year (1908) and I remember hearing a number of people remark on Bill's ability as a presiding officer. He was a regular John R. Mott, and had everything at his fingers' ends, everybody knowing just what meetings were to be held, and where, through his conciseness and clearness. All his correspondence beforehand, tentative programs, bills, etc., were kept in such orderly fashion that he never had to waste time looking for anything.

This same ability in handling affairs came out in our work together in the Yale Hope Mission. Bill gave a great deal of attention to it, though he did not let it interfere with his other work as far as I could see. He went down to the meetings a great deal, and might often be found in the lower parts of the city at night—on the street, in a cheap lodging-house or some restaurant to which he had taken a poor hungry fellow to feed him—seeking to lead men to Christ.

Yet his studies were not neglected, for in February of his junior year, when the list of those who had made Phi Beta Kappa was announced, Borden was one of thirty chosen, and when the society organized a little later, he was elected president for the coming year. In this connection, Charles Campbell recalled:

At the Phi Beta Kappa banquet, which came late in the winter of 1908, Bill as president of the society took the lead. The Phi Beta Kappa banquet is perhaps the finest of the yearly banquets given at Yale. Many celebrated men are invited from other colleges and most of the best known professors of the University itself, so that the dinner is quite an affair. I have a pleasant recollection of the dignified way in which Bill presided and made the opening address. It was a striking illustration of the maturity and balance of the man.

William Borden's college activities were summarized in the Yale Alumni Weekly as follows:

He was president of Phi Beta Kappa. In athletics he was active in football, baseball, crew and wrestling, rowing on the winning, 1909, club crew in the fall of junior year,[1] and playing on the winning Philosophical and High Oration baseball team and on the Phi Beta Kappa team. He served on the Class Book Committee and on the Senior Council. Elected a Class Deacon, he devoted himself largely to religious work. He was unwilling to join any fraternity or secret society, because he feared that it might set him apart from the body of the class.

---

[1] "One of the events of the regatta on Lake Whitney," wrote Mr. C. Campbell, "was a race between the four class crews. This was won by [the class of] 1909, Bill's class. I have before me the cup awarded to him for his part in this race. It is inscribed: 'Fall Regatta, 1907, Club Championship, won by 1909, W.W. Borden, Number four.'"

He accepted, however, an election to the Elihu Club.

Due to his newly elected office to the Senior Council, with its special relation to the faculty, and his duties on the Senior Class Book Committee, he found himself busier than ever. He was keenly interested in doing his full share of what one may think drudgery for the good of the class. He spent hours collecting from the class their votes for individual preferences. When the Class Book appeared, he was voted third for "the hardest worker," fourth among "the most energetic," ninth among "the most to be admired," and seventh in the vote for "the one who had done most for Yale"; this from a class of close to three hundred students.

But it was in the small, intimate meetings of the Student Volunteer Band that Borden was most himself, as one friend recalls:

> It was there the flame of his spiritual life seemed to glow most brightly. There reserve was thrown aside; he was among those who were in sympathy with his life-purpose. His presence in the Band kept the spiritual tone right up to concert pitch. . . . It will always be an inspiration to remember him there, in his true element.

"Of course the outstanding thing in one's memory of Bill is his missionary motive," wrote Dr. Kenneth Latourette. "He was so sane and unpretending about it, and yet it was so completely a part of his life. The memory of it and his courage to carry the gospel to unreached fields is a constant rebuke and inspiration to me. He had the Pauline spirit. I recall how he quoted him, about not wanting to build on another man's foundation (Romans 15:20, 21). The steadfastness of that purpose of Bill's had no small part, I am sure, in bringing the largest Volunteer Band in Yale's history into the days of his college life.

> How easy Bill was to pray with! He was a jolly fellow—loved a rough-house; delighted to get hold of a man and crack his ribs! He could be jolly with the rest, and when the crowd was gone it would be just as natural for him to say, "Come into the bedroom and let us have prayer together."
>
> There was no sense of incongruity about it. I remember very vividly—how could one ever forget—those times of prayer, when just the two of us would kneel down and take

to God some of the problems we were facing. Bill was so simple in his prayer life, so natural, so trustful! *He was the easiest man to pray with I have ever known.*

Prayer was to him his most important work, as well as the breath of his life. He had a card system for recording prayers and their answers in connection with individuals who were on his heart, and a loose-leaf notebook in which he listed subjects for prayer in groups, one for each day of the week. To take in the meaning of those notes even for one day is a revelation of the depth and thoroughness of the prayer life they represent, reaching out to the ends of the earth. It helps one to understand the statement made by his closest friend Campbell:

Through all the time I have known him, when there has been opportunity, we have never parted without going on our knees and praying for God's work.

It is easy to see how much this friendship must have meant to the two.[2] But there was nothing exclusive about it, any more than about Borden's religion. "Bill was to me the rarest Christian spirit I have ever known," was the estimate of one now on the faculty—and yet he was so very human too!

"No picture of Bill at New Haven would be complete," wrote Jefferson to another of the class deacons, "without the old slouch hat he used to wear so often. It was of brownish grey, pointed at the top, torn on the side, and with a large convenient hole used to hang it up by. One time I set fire to Bill's hat. When he discovered the flame he was suddenly active to rescue the treasure and punish me for my presumption." The hat, it may be added, was not discarded even after this fiery ordeal.

Mac Vilas, his roommate for two years at Yale, spoke of

---

[2]"Campbell prepared for Yale at Kingsley School and at the Montclair Military Academy. He got a Philosophical Oration appointment and is a member of Phi Beta Kappa; a member of the University track team for the last three years; he won his 'Y' in the pole vault in the inter-collegiate meet, sophomore year. Elected a Deacon, sophomore year, his chief interest in college has been Dwight Hall, of which he is president. He is an active Bible group leader. He served on the Class Day committee. Zeta Psi. Skull and Bones." *The history of the Class of 1909, Yale College.*

him as, "a Christian, first, last and all the time"; but he was interested in recalling details that showed that he was not narrow in his sympathies, and that socially as well as physically he was an all-round man.

In the letter he wrote accepting an invitation to be usher at Mac's wedding, Borden spoke about not being much for socializing though his social instinct was strong. He would seem to be comfortable in almost any situation.

Borden was very interested in business affairs. He read the *New York Times* regularly at College, and also read the *Wall Street Journal*. Fairly conversant with the stock quotations from day to day, he followed the big financial developments eagerly.

"Bill was very reticent about mentioning his financial affairs," wrote Vilas. "In fact, I don't remember ever asking him a single thing about them, as I considered it none of my business. This reticence was, to my mind, another indication that he would have been a shrewd businessman. He was able to keep his own counsel, to say little but think and work hard. Bill seemed to pay considerable attention to his Chicago business affairs, for he corresponded a good deal with Mr. Spink and I remember his mentioning several business trips to Chicago. . . .

"I believe I am right in saying that Bill was elected to every class office for which he was nominated, and I well remember one stormy class meeting—we could scarcely hear ourselves speak—when a word of suggestion from him brought order out of the chaos, and showed very clearly the quality of the fellows' respect and admiration for him."

Others also recall characteristics which impressed them of William Borden:

> No matter if some said he was too religious, or others that he was too narrow, or that he was heavy, there was one thing nobody at Yale ever questioned—that was that he was *strong*. He was red-blooded and he had the punch. He played hard and he studied hard and was intense in his religious beliefs. When he bucked the football line, every ounce of his hundred and seventy-five was back of him. When he was elected to the presidency of Phi Beta Kappa he received the highest

scholarship honor in Yale. There was power written all over him. You either followed him or you let him alone. . . . I can vouch that he was the strongest religious force in our class at Yale. —*Max Parry, a leading member of the class of 1909*

He certainly was one of the strongest characters I have ever known, and he put backbone into the rest of us at College, who were interested in the same things but did not have the strength he had. There was real iron in him, and I always felt he was of the stuff martyrs were made of, and heroic missionaries of more modern times. Our point of view differed on many things; but it was always refreshing to discuss matters with him even if we disagreed, because I knew so well his strength of purpose and consecration. I had complete trust in him as a man. . . . He never seemed to lose his vision for a single instant. . . . Among many fine qualities, the supreme impression he made upon others, it seems to me, was that of moral rectitude. —*John Magee, writing from China*

Bill was the great example to me of one who seemed to realize always that he must be about his Father's business, and not wasting time in the pursuit of amusement. . . . He was a man who had very high ideals and lived up to them; who impressed his sincerity upon you by his daily life among his fellows, no matter how restricting his beliefs might be. We disagreed about some things, and I thought Bill narrow, but as the years pass I am beginning to see that his perspective was the one which I am only just reaching. But I want to say that even when I disagreed with him, there was never a moment that I did not respect him for those same beliefs and the way in which he lived up to them. —*Farrand Williams*

In his sophomore year we organized Bible study groups and divided up the class of three hundred or more, each man interested taking a certain number, so that all might, if possible, be reached. The names were gone over one by one, and the question asked, "Who will take this person or that?" When it came to one who was a hard proposition there would be an ominous pause. Nobody wanted the responsibility. Then Bill's voice would be heard: "Put him down to me."

Thus he got together a group of the hardest to reach, the least attractive, and worked for them faithfully. In a house in College Street he had three of his incorrigibles, anything but promising material for a Bible class. I remember one meeting of the group when only one man was present, while another listened through a half-open door into the next room. But Bill held on, glad that they gave him the opportunity.

His rugged yet simple faith in Christ as Savior and Lord, and in the Bible as God's inspired Word, is a tonic to me, for one, whenever I am tempted to drift into barren doubtings or a purely intellectual attitude toward our faith. But with all his convictions as to the futility of higher criticism and his distrust of the so-called new theology, I cannot recall hearing him speak unkindly, or even frequently, of the many who preached it to us from the Yale pulpit or lecture desk. He was always the Christian gentleman. —*Dr. Kenneth Latourette*

There never was a time during those years when Bill was not looking for the opportunity of doing personal work. — *Charles Campbell*

Joe Twitchell's remark in our Deacons' meeting one night was interesting, as showing something of Bill's idea of personal work. Joe said, "Bill hunts up the worst skunk in college, and goes after him." —*E.F. Jefferson, Class Deacon and famous Yale first baseman*

One of the passions of his life was for righteousness. He had indeed that "hunger and thirst" we read about in Matthew 5:6. His prayer-life was full of petitions that illustrated this, and his actual living illustrated it too.

I remember, in this connection, that after we had finished our final examinations in College we had a four days' interval before Commencement, and Bill with a few others of us ran up to his place in Maine and attempted to sail his boat down to New Haven. We had head-winds all the way, and could do no better than reach Cape Cod and put in to Hyannisport in time to take a train to New Haven. As we walked up the streets of Hyannisport, where Bill had spent a summer as a boy, he remembered that at the close of that vacation he had gone away owing some shopkeeper in the place a few cents. He had forgotten all about it, but it came back to him as we walked up the street that day, and felt he must find the little shop and pay the debt, that he might be straight with the world. That was his nature all through. If he found anything wrong with his life, he set out to make it right.

Bill had a great loving heart, which always seemed to me his richest and rarest quality. There were many, perhaps, who, seeing him in a casual way busy with the work he had to do, set him down as severe and unapproachable. We knew that

the very opposite was true. He had one of the most affectionate, loveable natures of any man I have ever known. No one
who visited in his home could for a moment doubt this. But
I mean more than family love. He had a way, for example,
when walking with a friend, of putting his arm over his shoulder as they talked. I can feel the great loving touch of his arm
about my shoulder now.

After graduation we attended Northfield again, sleeping
in a tent as before. For two summers, at least, Bill waited at
table during the Conference. He never did this if there was a
man needing the job to help to make expenses. But if the coast
was clear, on would go the waiter's apron and he would do
the work, getting nothing to eat himself until the crowd had
left the diningroom. He never told me why he did this. It may
have been partly to keep friends company who had to wait
for monetary reasons. But I always felt it went deeper than
that, and that Bill was trying to be among us as "he that
serveth." —*Charles Campbell*

And lastly, from one of the early converts from Yale Hope
Mission, another insight to William Borden:

I came in here on the twenty-seventh of March, 1908. I
was on a drunk and hadn't much use for religion. I'm not
going to tell the worst part of my life, but I was a rambler all
right—a down-and-out bum. There was only three states in
the Union I hadn't been in. I had heard of the Mission, same
as a good many of them do. I knew it was the only thing that
would save me from booze. Well, I went out, that first night.
I had a Christian mother, and I got to thinking of her and I
came back. That was the twenty-ninth of March, and that
night Bill was here and he spoke to me. Bill was a great
personal worker. He always believed in getting right down
and talking to a man. If Bill had anything to say he gave it
right out. I know the gist of what he said to me that night:
"What are you going to do about it? Can't you see where
you've missed the road?"

He would tell you to hope again; tell you of the God who'd
made the universe and held you in the hollow of His hand and
could help you if you'd only ask. That's the way he talked.
He was one good boy. I could never forget him as long as I
breathe—no, I never forget him. And he was barely twenty
that night I first knew him! He was at Yale College here then,

and Luis Bernhardt was superintendent of the Mission.

I went forward and kneeled down and Bill came and kneeled down beside me, and he explained as much as he could the power of Jesus Christ, and how it was only Him who could help me. I never drank from that night to this, never felt like it—never felt like it, from that twenty-ninth day of March to this—and before that I was drunk most of the time. I had been drunk about all that winter. Bill was a great man to watch you and not say much, but just ask how you were getting along. Well, after I was converted I come every night—didn't miss a night after that for seven weeks. It's all fresh in my mind yet. I got work, too, soon. I got a job on an ice-wagon. That was one of the greatest tests on the booze question that a man ever got. I was boss of the team that year, and went back and was boss again the second summer. I was boss sixteen or seventeen months altogether. I hadn't worked only three weeks when they put me in charge of the team.

I saw Bill right along those times, except in his vacation; then he was in Europe. And he wrote me a letter. After some time I went back to the shop, and then I was foreman in the New Haven County Jail, where I'd served time in a cell. About two years after I was converted I was remarried right in this building, right up-stairs. I think Bill sent a letter that he couldn't come. He knew I was going to be married. He met my wife and family—seemed tickled to death, too, to meet 'em. We've got a home now in Yalesville, Connecticut, and a big garden, plenty of land, lots of chickens, and a piano in the house—makes quite a change from when I first came to the Mission drunk, with no prospects but whiskey! There's not been a day since my conversion that I haven't had money in my pocket, not a day from that day to this. God had wonderfully blessed me.

After my conversion I was baptized and joined the Church. If Bill hadn't opened this Mission I'd be dead. My old chum who was once on bums with me, he'd never have been converted if it hadn't been for this Mission. We was holding prayer meetings at different houses. They'd come in drunk sometimes. Then I always took 'em after the meetings and gave 'em a talking to just before thy left. Told 'em about this work here at Yale Hope Mission. There's no time in a drunkard's life when he don't have serious thoughts. When he drowns his conscience in booze, he's tearing away from the voice of God, I think. Well, someone asked my chum to come when the meeting was at my house. He said he would if Jack Clark would lead. He knew that what God did for Jack Clark He could do for him. There was about twenty-four there and I led, and that night Whitney Todd, my chum, was converted. He lives right in Yalesville now and is foreman of a shop. He's got his wife and children with him, and he's always got his hand out to the man that's down. So you see you cannot trance what Yale Hope Mission's done by what you see lying around. Not till the books of Heaven are opened will you know what Bill Borden done by opening Yale Hope Mission. . . .

He was great at individual work. As a talker, he'd hasten through his address and get to work with the men, always aiming to get close to the man he was talking with—always with his hand on his shoulder. He didn't believe in talking over peoples' heads, but tried to land right on his man and bring his thoughts right home. He would interest you quicker than the ordinary man, because he had a more sympathetic way to start in. He seemed to reach out and win you. I watched him from night to night, and always, as soon as the invitation was given to come forward, he would be off the platform and right down among the men, and he'd urge them to accept a better life. He was always sympathetic, and he never went at a man in the same way twice. He had a habit of putting his hand on a man's shoulder, and they'd most always break down when he spoke to them.

I never knew a feller just like Bill. I'd like to get a hold of one of his pictures. Seems to me if I saw one I'd 'most try to steal it. I never knew a feller like him. He was a gentleman in every sense of the word, and a Christian through and through. That was first and last in his life. He enjoyed life and people who came in contact with him, seeing his happy spirit, would say, "Why, life is worth living after all."

Why, the way he came amongst us, you would never think he was a man of wealth, and he always dressed so plain. He had a peculiar way, very interesting to me. He wouldn't tell you anything about himself, but he had a way of making you talk and tell things. It seemed to be his whole object, to know how I was and about my life so as he could help. It couldn't seem possible a man could be so humble and yet so great. He could talk to anyone, didn't matter who they was. And he'd get down with his arms round the poor burly bum and hug him up.

Never knowed his like in this world. I know he must have done for hundreds just what he done for me. He was always trying to study into the lives of men, to see how they'd work out and how he could help 'em.

It was Professor Henry Wright who said, "It is my firm conviction that the Yale Hope Mission has done more to convince all classes of men at Yale of the power and practicability of Christianity to regenerate individuals and communities than any other force in the University."

10

RESTING IN THE SPIRIT

1906–1912

Age 18–24

No duty could overtask him,
No need his will outrun;
Or ever we could ask him
His hands the work had done.

—J. G. Whittier

Borden loved the sea, and was at home on it and in it. Most of his vacations during student years were spent at Camden, Maine, where he almost lived on the white-sailed *Tsatsawassa*. Talking with the captain of the yacht one day, who knew and loved him as did few others, Mrs. Borden remarked:

"You at any rate must have seen him off duty—off his guard."

"Mrs. Borden," was the unexpected reply, "William was never off his guard."

It was a true word, for in spite of all the good times, in the midst of them, he was steadfast in his commitment to the Lord. This comes out in the recollections of those who shared both in his merriment and work. A medical-student friend wrote:

> There were few things that Bill liked better than to put on his canvas jeans and jumper and sit behind the tiller of his

yacht in a brisk breeze. Many a pleasant sail I have had with
Bill, and many a time we have been together in sloppy
weather. One well-remembered summer we took a cruise
down the Nova Scotia shore, and there is no time like a cruise
for getting to know one another. Bill was our skipper and an
ideal one, but he didn't stop at being in charge. There were
few meals we ate that he hadn't cooked. Life on the boat was
full of joy from beginning to end with Bill to keep things
going.

One morning we were becalmed in the middle of the Bay
of Fundy. It was a hot sultry day, and we had been talking
about sharks. Suddenly Bill said, "Sharks or no sharks, here
goes!" And he was overboard in a moment, swimming round
the yacht.

One learned in those days more of the secret of Bill's life,
that his strength lay in his prayer-life. No matter what the
weather might be, he would always hand over his trick at the
wheel and go below for his times of quiet. I remember him
distinctly one very rough day, with the boat standing on her
beam-end, coming below and climbing up on his berth and
losing himself in his God.

Mrs. Henry W. Frost, who had chaperoned a merry house-
party on the yacht, wrote:

The time I came to know him best was on the cruise we
had in August 1911. I cannot think of an instance during those
seven days of good thorough testing in close quarters, when
William did not put everyone's comfort and pleasure before
his own. He was captain and steersman, steward and cook for
a party of ten hungry people, and well he did it. It was something more than the salt sea air that made his coffee and tea
and corned-beef hash and pancakes so popular.

Between times he was ready for any game. Stretched out
in the cockpit at dominoes, his hearty laugh rang out with any
success that was achieved.

On Sunday we went to morning service ashore, and in the
evening as we finished our meal and had a sing, with perfect
naturalness and simplicity he led in a brief prayer service. It
was always a pleasure to me to have him conduct prayers. His
scripture reading, while reverent, was so natural and his prayers so direct and simple, conveying the feeling that God was
near and real.

Charles Campbell recalled the happy days at Camden:

Three weeks of one summer and the larger part of another
I was with Bill Borden. That time, spent largely out of doors,
opened my eyes to Bill's real self even more than had close
association with him at College. At Yale I had learned that he
was a rare man to work with; our weeks together in his summer
home showed me that he was a rare man indeed to spend
recreation time with. At College I knew, as did all his friends,
the strength and intensity of the serious purpose of his life;
our happy, every-day comradeship at Camden taught me more
of his very human and loveable boyishness, and his enjoyment
of outdoor life and play. There was no mistaking the fact that
Bill liked to sail, that he liked to swim, play tennis and golf.
His laugh was always the heartiest, his enthusiasm the most
contagious, and his delight at doing well the most evident.

One of our sailing trips was from Camden to Beverley
Farms, on the Massachusetts north-shore. We had hardly
rounded the lighthouse at the entrance to Camden harbor when
we realized that a stiff breeze was blowing. A few hours later,
with Monhegan Island astern, we were facing the full force
of the open ocean. By six P.M. we were off Portland and,
with wind and rainstorms becoming more frequent, held a
consultation as to whether we should run for shelter. Just then
a coaster, which had been wallowing southward, emerged
from a squall, her top-sail and top-mast gone, and, changing
her course, ran for Portland Harbour. That decided Bill; but
his decision was that, having started for Beverley, to Beverley
we would go. Through the stormy night that followed, Bill
was quiet and self-possessed, and I remember that when he
took his turn at the wheel his strength and confidence seemed
an assurance that all would be well. Serious though the situation was, Bill could laugh when he sang out to us at midnight
that the lines with which we had been towing our power-
dinghy had parted, taking pleasure in fighting the battle out
with only our own resources to depend on.

Some of my most vivid recollections of Bill cluster round
those different sailing trips. They range from the above experience to the spectacle of Bill in rough weather, seated in
the cabin, calmly disposing of quantities of Grapenuts and
condensed milk. Great was our secret admiration for one who
could perform such a feat at a time when the rolling of the

boat had put some of us *hors de combat*.

I remember one evening anchoring off Bar Harbour about seven o'clock. By the time all was ship-shape, the sun had set and the riding lights were shining from all the boats in the harbor. Before getting supper, Bill suggested that we have a swim. The air was chilly, and the black water rippling by with the outgoing tide looked colder than I had ever seen it. But overboard we went, swam a few strokes, took another dive, and were out again and dressing. The splendid reaction put us in the best of spirits as we prepared supper. I can see Bill now, hustling round that cabin, whistling, singing, just full of the joy of living.

It was that same time, I think, that we sat on the deck talking of another trip when we had put into Bar Harbour after sailing the entire preceding night. We had anchored at about the same spot, and as soon as possible had turned in for a little sleep. Before long we had wakened to find the boat dragging her anchor and almost upon the rocks. I can feel Bill's hearty slap upon my back and hear his laughter still, as we recalled how we had had to hustle to get out of danger.

Another experience happened off the coast of Massachusetts. They had been watching a school of whales blowing some distance away. A few moments later one of them lazily came to the surface, not a hundred feet from their fifty-foot yacht. In some alarm one of the party called to Bill, who was at the wheel, to keep the boat off. His response was to edge in a little nearer, with—"Oh, let's have a good look!"

He was brushing up his Greek, the summer of his graduation from Yale, with a view to the entrance examination at Princeton. Out in the yacht he would often go below and study Greek. He did a great deal of studying aboard his boat during the years Charlie knew him, and was diligent at making the odd moments count.

One day we sailed over to Eagle Island to take part in races that were being run. The wind was very light, and we came to the starting-line just after the race had begun. There was no time to report to the judges to enter and no time to put the tender ashore. Bill managed everything. We hauled the tender up on deck and went after the boats that had already started. All through the race Bill was captain, giving his orders and making every point to get the most out of his boat. We were heeled far over most of the time, as a good wind had sprung up. It all resulted in our crossing the winning line well in the lead. We were not allowed the victory, because we had not reported beforehand, but the winning was just as real all the same.

Sailing and tennis with Bill were always great fun, but the best hours of our visits were passed in quite another way. Before going to Camden a friend had wonderfully opened the Bible to me, giving me a new insight into its content. I mentioned this to Bill, and he at once suggested further Bible-study together. It had been good to relax and have fun with him, but to join him in the one thing nearest his heart was worth incomparably more.

It was not only to his guests that Borden's life meant much during the summer vacations. Many residents in Camden and the vicinity looked forward to his coming, and through his friendship some found Christ and a transformed life.

Among those was the gardener, a valuable employee of the family, who had begun to drink heavily. Mrs. Borden had done all she could to help him, but without success, and one day when she was away from home he was found drunk near the house. The next morning he sent a note to William saying that he was ill and could not come to work, a situation which was explained by Melanie, the children's former nurse, who had found him. Waiting only to have her pray with him about the visit, William set out to see the gardener. But when he reached the house it was only to be told that he did not feel like seeing anyone that day.

"I know the reason," William said to his wife. "Please ask him to let me come in."

The talk that followed resulted in a transformation that brought blessing to the whole family. A new life began for the man that day, and months later William was writing from college, "Your gardener is a constant source of joy and thanksgiving to God, is he not?"

But of all his Camden friends it was Captain Arey who knew Borden best and to whom his life meant most. The following recollections are given just as they came from his heart:

I've known him ever since he first come to Camden, and that must have been about nine years ago. If anyone showed on their outside the happiness of being a Christian it was Mr. Borden. When he talked it just seemed as if you could feel his earnestness.

When we two was out alone—we went all the way to New Haven alone once—I have seen him kneel for perhaps an hour at a time and never lift his head. The villagers loved him, everybody loved him. He was so noble-looking! When he came up in the spring, he always shook hands with everybody. All the summer-people don't do that. If 'twas a stranger or a fisherman, didn't make no difference. He always spoke to everybody, like as if he wanted to, and shook hands with them.

William was a nice hand to sail a boat. You didn't need no one else when he was along. I used to be afraid he'd fall in the water, at first. He was always singing and jumping around. He'd climb away up the riggin' and get into the row-boat behind. He did everything he tried to do well. He was so strong, too! When he'd go out and work at the riggin', I'd be afraid he'd break the sail, he was so strong. Sometimes he'd steer and sometimes he'd help with the sails, but he was an expert on the boat. He could take a chart and go anywhere with it. Of course, he'd studied into it and learned it. It didn't seem hard for him to go through with anything he undertook— it just seemed easy.

One awful good feature he had; if the boat wasn't fixed up quite as it ought to be, perhaps if ladies came aboard and the brass wasn't cleaned, I'd tell him about it, and he'd smile and say it was all right. He never spoke a cross word to me all the time I was with him.

He lent me two books by Gordon, *Talks on Prayer* and *Talks on Power*. We have a Young Peoples' Meeting in the Baptist Church here. After the summer in London when he was converted, he would sometimes lead our prayer-meeting. If I had the job, I'd get him to do it for me. Others did too, for they liked to hear him. He could always hold the audience. Sometimes the young people are a little noisy at their meeting, but they was still when he spoke.

Sometimes he'd tell us he was going to be a missionary— seemed to think he was mapped out for it. If 'twas worldly pleasure he'd wanted, he could have had everything. But he was so much different from others! All his pleasure seemed to be in going about doin' people good. The last summer here at one of the meetings he said he was goin' to the Muslims.

He spoke about the National Bible Institute one night, but I don't remember just what he said.

If we was out all night on the boat, he'd roll in the blanket and sleep on deck. The others would be in the cabin. There might be a bed to spare, but he'd take the deck. He liked it better.

One summer here, he and Mr. T. held open-air meetings. They'd begin right in front of the hotel, about 7:30, and get the crowds sort of interested. They had a little organ and would sing. William could sing quite well. He had a strong voice. Then they'd go into the Opera House, which they'd rented for a while. Sometimes it was crowded full. The last two evenings they'd have after-meetin's, and many stayed. After the meeting was opened—in the Opera House—anybody could speak. Many did. The superintendent of the mills spoke one night, and sometimes ministers would come and speak.

It was blowin' awful heavy one night—dark and rainy. Two other fellers was out with us, his friends. About two o'clock in the morning, the bran' new boat we was towin', the steam-launch, rolled over and sunk, the rope parted. I remember what he said.

"The boat's gone," he called down to the other fellers. "We can go faster now!"

Lots and lots of boats that night that was about as big as the *Tsatsawassa* was wrecked—that is, the sails were torn and the spars broke, so that they had to be towed in. The storm commenced about eleven o'clock. James Perry and another of William's friends was with us. I don't think any of us slept. I know I didn't, and I know William didn't. It was about six o'clock next morning when we got into Beverly Farms and anchored (after a record run of nearly two hundred miles in eighteen hours). When all was made safe, William said: "Now we'll have family prayers, and give thanks for gettin' in."

He always had prayers for us every mornin'. Whoever was on the boat, we always had prayers and a blessin' at table. Sometimes she'd be so keeled over that we'd be standin' up, but that didn't make no difference. We always had a blessin'. If we was in port Sunday mornin', we'd go ashore to church. Perhaps I'd stay aboard—someone had to be there. But before he'd go ashore, he'd have prayers with me on the boat. He

was always thoughtful, that way, of others. If he'd been my
own brother he couldn't have used me any better.

Once he and Mary was out, and a fog and heavy sea came
on. We couldn't get back to the landing stage, so they went
to my house and stayed all night. He just said so natural-like
to my wife:

"Have you anything to eat? We didn't get much supper!
Can you give us some milk and cake?"

My wife went to all the meetin's. She likes him, too. He
wasn't like one of the summer people! I'd be awful glad to
have his picture, so'd my wife.

When he and I'd go out alone sometimes, I'd ask where
he'd like to go.

"Anywhere," he'd say, "so as to get out where it's quiet."

And he'd go down into the cabin with his Bible or some
other book and study all the time we was out. It might be
three hours or so. And when we'd come in, he seemed to be
kind of refreshed in his mind.

He always read the Bible before turnin' in at night. It
didn't matter who was there. If I was alone with him, he'd
read it to me and explain it. Yes, he was jolly and he was
happy in the work he was undertakin'.

Other recollections of his years at Princeton come from the
family of his college friend, Sherwood Day. The Days were
fortunate in having a camp of their own, tucked away on the
low shoulder of a mountain overlooking Lake George. William
loved the spot, close to that exquisite expanse of water, and
loved still more the Christian fellowship recalled in the following letters from Mrs. Day and two of her daughters, Bryn Mawr
students:

In the very first conversation I ever had with Bill, we
discovered that we both believed in the inerrancy of the Bible,
and I can feel yet the hearty grasp of his outstretched hand as
we laughed in serious sympathy over our common orthodoxy!
That was the summer he joined us at Shelving Rock. I had
hesitated to invite him, because it was real camping, and I
fancied he might need some conveniences which are no longer
considered luxuries but necessaries. I soon learned, however,
that comforts were easily dispensable with him, and that no

change of surroundings interfered with his habitual walk with God.

That same summer, Harriet our daughter was with us. She dubbed Bill "the Parson," but you cannot know the amused little smile with which he responded to her fun. They spent so many happy times together that I remember Sherwood saying: "I wish the College fellows could see this side of Bill!"

We knew that he went in for athletics and outdoor life, but until then it seemed as if even they were *serious* undertakings. But with Harriet, the playful side was brought out, and we were so glad to know the *boy* under the manly exterior.

I, too, loved his standing simply and firmly for the eternal verities of our faith. That staunchness of his, after all his thought and study, has meant much to me. And I have learned much, too, from *the way* Bill stood for truth. We always noticed that the more earnest he became, the lower, not the louder, he spoke. When others in argument would raise their voices, he would grow more quiet and speak softer, resulting in everyone listening.

I recall one day a somewhat heated discussion of the suffrage question. We finally got down to Genesis, Mother basing her plea against it on the teachings of that book, upon which one of our pro-suffrage guests denied much belief in Genesis, anyway. I don't remember that up to that point Bill had said much, but somehow, the first thing I knew, he was talking along and the other guests were listening. We all listened. Much that he said was beyond us. We did not know enough to follow it fully. But the impression was made that there is such a thing as a deep scholarly conviction as to the authority and inspiration of the book (Genesis) and that the speaker was no unthinking conservative, but an intelligent believer in the Bible.

I do not know that he convinced the friends in question. They did not talk long. But he did what I felt at the time was perhaps more needed, showed that we could hold to the old views in these matters, after thinking. Real certainty and security in the truth *is* unruffled when the attack comes. He was so sure, as on that occasion, of what he believed—Him whom he believed—that he did not get excited and loudly insist on his opinions. He could wait to say what he *knew*. And the more you knew him the more sure you felt that, keen and active as his intellect was, that knowledge was the result of no mere theological training, but of personal experience, and prayerful Spirit-guided study of the Word of God.

The thought of him always challenges me. I mean that one knew that he was holding himself and always would hold himself to what he felt to be best and highest. He would not stoop to petty excuses or take advantage of loopholes for self-indulgence. Here at camp he was up early for his Morning Watch as regularly as, I am sure, he must have been at the Seminary. I can see his Testament coming out of his pocket now! As surely as he carried that Testament he carried his religion. You felt he would never be one to want a vacation from religious duties. They were not "duties" to him. It was just *natural* to him to take that morning hour for fellowship with God, and he bore its imprint all through the day.

It was always an opportune time with Bill to speak of the deepest things, because with him they were the realest things. His spiritual life affected all his living, the heartiness and wholesomeness of his fun as well as his religious activities. . . . If there arose in his mind a doubt about the rightness of something, he put the doubtful thing aside at once. For example, he became much interested in a card game someone was playing here in camp and took some share in it. Then, one day he would not play it any more, and you knew he had questioned the rightness of his taking such a keen interest in the game and had shut down on it immediately. It was this steadfast turning from doubtful things that gave him, I think, the atmosphere of separateness that was part of his power.

And then, I suppose, this single-mindedness in his spiritual life was the secret of that fixity of purpose which took him straight along whither he had set out. What Bill started, you might be quite sure he would finish. From the room in which I write I can see where a limb had been cut off a tree, high up from the ground. He cut it off. Someone had expressed a wish that the dead limb might go, because it looked like an ugly clenched fist, and he set out to do it. The ladder was not long enough and he had to prop it up—it was on a steep hillside, and almost dangerous to do so. He had to hang on with his right arm and saw with his left, in an almost impossible position. I can see him doing it now, sawing and resting and sawing again, but sticking at it until the limb fell.

One other thing I want to speak of, but I don't quite know what to call it. It was something that made you feel that everything would be all right as long as he was around. It was partly, I suppose, his consideration for others.

When, one evening last September, we ran down to the Sagamore, to take him there to get an automobile for Lake George, he discovered that we had no flashlight in the launch with which to examine the engine if necessary. He insisted upon giving us his, one from his travelling bag, because he felt we ought not to be without it. And as we started home, leaving him there on the dock, he called out to Rosalie and me—novices at running the engine—not to forget about an oil-cup, I think it was, that it was important we should attend to.

He was such a one to rely on! And it seemed to me that His Lord's spirit of service had so permeated his life that it not only led him to set his face to the field of greatest need, but meanwhile made his life full of *little services*, day by day, that many would not see the occasion for. It was easy to see his force, his devotion to Christ's cause, but it was only after having him around that you began to appreciate what a Christlike man he was.

. . . A kindness he did in a New York station is one of the things I have recalled repeatedly. We were going out to take a train, when I noticed that he had dropped behind, and turning, I saw him helping a very poor immigrant woman who was struggling along with many bundles and a baby in her arms. How well I remember, at camp, how he used to stand near the kitchen door and watch for a chance to be of use. We often said that the table was never cleared so quickly as when Bill did it.

And what a help he was in some German I had to do (for an examination at Bryn Mawr)! The days at camp were pretty well filled with picnics, canoeing, swimming, etc., and it was not easy to make time for study. He was anxious that I should finish that German reading. If a thing had to be done, it was his way to do it and then put it from his mind. When there were a few minutes before it was time to start on a picnic or other outing he would say: "Can't we get some of that German done now?" I do not know how I should ever have "tackled" it without this encouragement. His help during the few days he was there gave me, so to speak, "a running start," and I was able to finish it in the required time. . . .

But with all his seriousness there was abundant playfulness and love of fun. He had an inexhaustible store of tricks, which kept us entertained many an evening. . . .

And one other thing about Bill—his instant and full obedience to the will of God. There never seemed to be any conflict in his life between duty and pleasure, for the moment he saw what his duty was, he did it. There was no procrastination about him. If the thing was hard to do, it made no difference. Feelings were out of the reckoning. "Obedience irrespective of feeling" was, perhaps, the strongest thing about his life.

One of the most vivid memories I have of him is as he sat before our open fire at camp one Sunday evening. We were all there singing hymns, and the only light was that of the fire which shone full on his face. How earnest it was, and with what joyousness he sang the hymns he loved best! "O Love that Will Not Let Me Go" and "In the Secret of His Presence" were among his favorites. But it was not the firelight only that brought that light to his face. These lines come to me as I recall the scene and especially that look of joy and calm:

Beautiful now his face had grown,
But the beauty was something not his own;
A solemn light from that blessed land
Within whose border he soon must stand.

"His ideals and ambitions were so great," wrote Elsa Frost, a young nurse in a hospital, "that anyone who knew him at all could not but be influenced by them, and to us who counted ourselves friends of his they were much more.

"My most vivid remembrance of William has not to do with any football game or sailing, but with a communion service we all attended together at Camden. I somehow think of him most often then—not that he did or said anything to fix it in my mind, but just that he seemed to be so in the spirit of the service. When at times I am tempted to wonder whether the end in view is worth all the work and struggle, just to remember the separations and hardships he was facing is enough to start me on again."

PART III

PRINCETON SEMINARY

Many crowd the Savior's kingdom,
Few receive His Cross.
Many seek His consolation,
Few will suffer loss,
For the dear sake of the Master,
Counting all but dross.

Many sit at Jesus' table,
Few will fast with Him,
When the sorrow-cup of anguish
Trembles to the brim:
Few watch with Him in the garden
Who have sung the hymn.

But the souls who love Him truly
Both in woe and bliss,
These will count their very heart's blood
Not their own but His!
Savior, Thou who thus hast loved me,
Give me love like this.

—Selected

11

WISDOM AND KNOWLEDGE

1909–1912

Age 21–24

The purpose of his life had been "to turn many to righteousness." The Bible was the source of all his power. He learned it, he loved it, he lived it. It made him what he was. And I am hearing from all parts of the world testimonies from men and women who were drawn to give their lives to the Savior through his teaching. That is a noble purpose to live for, is it not?

—Written of the Rev. Prebendary Webb Peploe,
  by his widow

Borden's life at Princeton was strenuous almost beyond belief, for in addition to his studies, he had many other responsibilities. He was now of age and had a big share in the management of large financial interests. His mother had come to live at Princeton, partly in order for his younger sister to see as much of him as possible. Their home was a center of hospitality, and as Mrs. Borden was still far from strong, William kept account of the household accounts as well as maintaining his responsibilities as host. His studies were absorbing, even more so than he had anticipated, and the pressure of other interests was not allowed to encroach upon the time they demanded. All this meant a heavy schedule and exercise of self-discipline.

He decided to take a full load of courses at Princeton Seminary largely due to the many unanswered questions that he had during his senior year at Yale. When urged to return as graduate secretary of the Y.M.C.A. he exclaimed to a college friend, "Gee whiz! I want to pull out for a while and see where I am. I must take time for thought and study rather than rush on in the same sort of activities."

So honest and earnest a nature could not be satisfied with uncertainty in the most vital issues. Three years of close mental application was a price he willingly paid for the strength that comes from knowledge and settled convictions. He was, at the same time, enlarging his missionary outlook by a special course of study for his Yale M.A. This had been gone over in detail with Professor Harlan P. Beach, before leaving college. The professor wrote:

> The ground covered was enough Arabic to secure the degree if offered alone, and in addition a broad course of missionary reading, mostly having to do with the science of missions, Muslim and missionary biographies. He was duly entered as a graduate student with permission to pass his examinations at his convenience. Had he done so, he would have covered more that even the best Master's Degree men are required to take. "Factors in Missionary Efficiency" was the theme decided upon for his thesis.

Borden did not share the view expressed by some Student Volunteers that it will be time enough when they reach the mission field to study missions. Even amid the pressure of college and seminary life he was following out a steady course of missionary reading, which made him always interesting and helpful at the band meeting and gave definiteness to his prayers. There was nothing half-done about his preparation. It was deep and thorough.

His friend Campbell wrote:

> Thus Bill entered upon three years of busy, happy life at Princeton. The studies were absorbing and the social life congenial. He was a member of the Benham Club, the oldest

eating club of the seminary. He played most of the games, but
was especially fond of tennis. He was a leader among the
Student Volunteers and was always present at the early morning prayer service of the Band each Wednesday.

In addition to the duties and pleasures that centered about
his life in the Seminary, Bill had many responsibilities outside
Princeton itself. In the fall of 1909 he had been made a trustee
of the Moody Bible Institute in Chicago. In the spring of 1910
he was appointed a delegate to the Edinburgh Missionary Conference by the China Inland Mission, and in the fall was made
one of the directors of the National Bible Institute of New
York City. He also became a member of the North American
Council of the China Inland Mission and of the American
Committee of the Nile Mission Press.

It is easy to see that the calls on his time would be many.
Few men of his age could have handled the duties that pressed
upon him so well. His singleness of purpose helped him and
gave such direction to his life that no one, even among his
nearest friends, saw anything but a quiet, consistent, unhur-
ried doing of each task that came. Almost every month he
went to New Haven to look over the work of the Yale Hope
Mission. The unusual feature of his relationship to all such
organizations was that he was never satisfied with merely
giving generous financial aid. In addition, he always gave
time, thought and counsel, usually conducting a service at the
Mission when he went to New Haven. New York, New Haven
and Chicago trips succeeded one another, and still he never
seemed to neglect his work, though he carried a much heavier
schedule than the average man. More than this, he stood very
high in scholarship.

Life at Princeton was highlighted by the happy home influences that surrounded him. The Borden home was hospit-
ably open to all. Students, missionaries and prominent lay
workers were frequent visitors. The tennis court, back of the
house, was the scene of many hotly contested games. In spite
of his busy schedule, Bill made it a point to get an hour's
exercise daily if it was possible. His eyes would light up at
the prospect of a good game of tennis. Back from class he
would rush to quickly change into tennis clothes and then out
to the court. He was never more than an average tennis player,
but he played hard all the time and gave his opponent a good
workout.

It is interesting to see from letters written only a little later the impression Borden made upon members of the faculty during those full years at Princeton.

"I never saw, perhaps, a finer example of a sound mind in a sound body," recalled Professor Brenton Greene. "I used to think as I saw him from my study window dashing down Library Place on his bicycle to the early morning recitations, 'that man is so strong and so sane that his prospect of life is better than that of any other student in our Seminary.'

"His memory was as wax to receive an impression and as marble to retain it. He had the happy faculty of seeing at once the gist of a question and going straight to the point. Yet he never relied on this power, but used every means at his command. Rarely if ever was he absent from the classes, and I cannot recall a single instance of inattention on his part. As might have been expected, he attained the natural result. He became distinguished as a scholar. . . . I well remember my deep regret, the feeling of positive loss, at the time of his graduation, when I read his last paper, knowing that I should never have another from him."

"No student has exerted a greater personal influence over me than did William Borden," wrote Professor Charles Erdman. "This was due both to the fact of our intimate friendship and to his peculiarly strong and impressive personality. His judgment was so unerring and so mature that I always forgot there was such a difference in our ages. His complete consecration and devotion to Christ were a revelation to me, and his confidence in prayer a continual inspiration.

"He had doubtless inherited unusual gifts, but these were developed by the most careful and persistent discipline, requiring great determination and fixity of purpose. . . . There was much in his life to tempt him to less strenuous work, to lure him to self-indulgence and content with imperfect achievement. There was also the test of resolution that comes from apparently conflicting duties. His responsibilities were great, his days crowded with a multiplicity of demands. Neither social duties, however, nor filial duties, nor the duties of Christian stewardship were allowed to draw him from the supreme duty

of preparation for his chosen work. The strain of unremitting
application was relieved by a keen sense of humor and a delight
in the society of relatives and friends. His friendship was one
of the most stimulating with which I have been blessed."

"It was as his teacher in Church History that I knew him
best," said Dr. John de Witt. "His fidelity, high intelligence
and rare grasp of the subjects brought before him made on me
a deep impression. But it was his spiritual ideal of life, his
absolute loyalty to it, the sound judgment he showed in ac-
tualizing it, not only in the choice of his work and field, but in
the details of daily activity and the simplicity and sincerity of
his character, that led me not only to respect but to reverence
him. I have had a few students among the many I have taught
who have distinctly called into action this feeling of reverence,
and he was one of them."

A similar note is found in not a few other letters from men
of experience and Christian standing. Dr. Henry W. Frost, for
example, Director in North America of the China Inland Mission, invited Borden, when only twenty-two, to a seat on its
Council. They had been in correspondence for years, and Dr.
Frost, who knew him personally, felt no hesitation in asking
him to become one of the burden-bearers at the heart of the
mission, sharing the prayer and faith as well as the problems
of those responsible for its direction.

"The disparity in age was seldom noticed," he recalls.
"There was an equality of mind which made him one with
those with whom he was associated. None could help noticing
the freshness of thought and enthusiasm of spirit characteristic
of youth, and the council rejoiced in these. But they were not
accompanied by immaturity of judgment. When he spoke, it
was evident that he was thinking carefully and broadly. He was
a constant illustration of the fact that it is no vain thing for a
man, even a young man, to obey the injunction 'If any of you
lack wisdom let him ask of God.' Christ, through the study of
the Word and through prayer, was made unto him 'wisdom.'
His advice, therefore, was sought by not a few who, in the
average case, would have gone to the man of more years. And
he seldom failed of help. If he did fail, his eagerness to be of

assistance made him a greater help than the average man would have been, though more wise through experience.''

Borden's love for the faith principles of the China Inland Mission was strong. He owed not a little in the deeper things of the spiritual life to his friendship with Dr. Frost, whose love for him was almost that of a father for a son. William had long consulted him in matters of importance, and especially as to his prospective relations with the mission. In this connection, Dr. Frost continued:

> The first time William Borden spoke to me about offering himself to the China Inland Mission was while he was in his sophomore year at Yale. He had already come to feel that his work should be in China and desired to put himself in a position to reach that land. But I felt he was then too young to come to a positive conclusion as to the country in which he should serve, and I advised him to postpone considering the matter.
>
> At the end of his university course he again consulted me about going to China. Once more I advised him to defer the decision, and urged him to prepare himself further by taking the seminary course at Princeton. This he did, with credit to himself and to the Seminary.
>
> Toward the end of his studies at Princeton, he again offered himself to the Mission for work in China. This time I was persuaded that God was indeed in the matter of his application. But to further test him, I asked if he had considered offering himself to the Presbyterian Board rather than to us. He replied that he had; that he highly esteemed the Presbyterian Board, but that there were three reasons why he was more drawn to the China Inland Mission—firstly, on account of its inter-denominational character; secondly, because of its emphasis upon evangelistic work; and thirdly, because it held to the belief in the personal and pre-millennial coming of Christ. So at last we considered his application and accepted him for service in China.

This was only ten days before Borden's graduation from Princeton, so that he had already been for more than two years a member of the council. It was an unusual coincidence when his case came up for final consideration and, as a candidate, he had to be asked to withdraw while the council proceeded to accept one of its own members as a probationary member of the mission.

But all this took place gradually, while the busy years at Princeton were passing on. During his first summer vacation from the seminary, Borden went to Europe, as we have seen, representing the China Inland Mission at the Ecumenical Missionary Conference in Edinburgh (1910), where he was the youngest of two thousand delegates. It was there that Mrs. Borden learned for the first time that his decision was taken to give himself definitely to work with Muslims in China, if that proved to be the Lord's will. Miss Annie Van Sommer had arranged for a gathering of representative workers from Muslim lands at the house where she was staying. Dr. Zwemer was chairman, and Mr. Gairdner and Dr. St. Clair Tisdall, all from Cairo, were there. In order to introduce people to one another, Dr. Zwemer asked each to rise and give his or her name and field. When Borden's turn came, he mentioned without hesitation that his prospective field was the Muslims of northwest China.

The summer was full. The missionary gatherings in Edinburgh were followed by a brief visit to Norway with Mr. Robert P. Wilder, who was then working among students in England and the rest of Europe. Of Borden's stay in their Norwegian home Mr. Wilder wrote:

> He took a real interest in our home-life and all our doings. He helped the children to learn to ride their bicycles, running by each of them in turn. Mrs. Wilder specially remembers how, when a box of aerated water had come by train and she was thinking of sending to the station for it, we saw to our surprise William Borden coming up the steep hill with the box on his shoulder. . . . He and I had long talks over God's Word and work, frequently pausing to pray about the matter we were discussing. He seemed never out of sight of the Mercy Seat.

A week in the Engadine gave Borden the conquest of peaks of both the Piz Pallu and the Piz Julier as glorious memories, and a few days at Lucerne brought delightful conversations with Mr. and Mrs. Charles Campbell, who were there on their honeymoon. They recalled:

He joined us in Lucerne. There were also a young Irishman and his bride in the same Pension, and for several days we five had a great time! We went to the Glacier Garten; went rowing on the lake and swimming in it, and altogether acted like a bunch of kids. Our afternoon teas were a wonderful mixture of assorted cakes and unlimited cups of tea.

Three weeks in Hanover were given to intensive study of German and opened Borden's eyes to threatened dangers. To Dr. Frost he wrote:

Hanover, July 20, 1910

Only today I read in a London paper "*Unity of Christendom—Gigantic Task!* Twenty-four American Episcopalians have undertaken to bring about a union of Christians all over the world—Protestants, Greek Orthodox, Roman Catholics, everybody, everywhere!" Things are certainly rushing to the climax. I wonder what will come next?

On the voyage home he was deep in Arabic with a view to the advanced course he was taking in that language and Aramaic. "I spent most of my time in London buying books," he wrote to his friend Campbell, "and am taking home a small library of theological and Oriental literature."

Back in Princeton he threw himself as before into all the religious and other activities of seminary life. Letters from many of his classmates might be quoted, but the following from the Rev. James M'Cammon, missionary to China, gives an impression of his influence:

His thoroughness, especially in his studies, was evident to us all. He kept up his work from day to day, so that he was not "rushed" as many of us were when examinations came around. So well did he have his knowledge in hand that long before the three hours' period for an exam was over he would have finished his paper and handed it in, to the approval of his fellow-students. It was my habit to look in on a classmate in Alexander Hall daily, and there, two or three afternoons in the week, I was sure to find Bill Borden and his friend, Mr. Fowler, doing extra-curriculum work on Arabic. On one such occasion I discovered that they had formed the project of making an Arabic concordance of the Bible, and had actually begun work upon it. I had known of their studiousness before, but this more than astonished me.

He was one of the most faithful attendants we had at the Y.M.C.A. and Student Volunteer meetings in the Seminary. He took his turn in leading such meetings, and his messages were of a devotional and missionary character that evidenced thorough preparation of mind and heart. One term he undertook to go through the Reports of the World's Missionary Conference which he had attended in Edinburgh, giving them in the form of a resume week by week. Those talks I shall never forget. His mastery of the facts was astonishing. He gave us in clear, condensed statements, from carefully prepared notes, a synopsis of each of these Reports, bringing out the spiritual bearing of the facts dealt with. It was a remarkable evidence of his knowledge as well as zeal in connection with foreign missions. . . .

He was a convinced believer in the personal and premillennial coming of our Lord. He looked for that glorious Advent as the hope of the Church and the only hope for the world. I often had conversations with him on this subject, and the extent of his knowledge and intensity of his convictions left their mark on my mind. One of my most prized possessions is a book on the Lord's Coming he once gave me as we were talking together.

Another conviction that dominated his life was that the Bible, from first to last, is the inspired Word of God. To him it was the Book of books. He had not only an intellectual grasp of its teachings such as one may get in a theological seminary, but he had the spiritual understanding of it which only comes through prayerful and devotional study in humble dependence on the Spirit of God. . . .

The secret of William Borden's life, as it seems to a fellow-student, was his belief in the sufficiency and abiding presence of the Lord Jesus Christ. For this was more than a belief, it was with him an experimental reality.

This reality and the strength he derived daily from his study of the Word of God made him feel intensely the drift away from these things in modern university life, a subject upon which he had written to Mr. Wilder, as leader of the Student Volunteer Movement, in the hope of inducing him to return to America:

Princeton, January 29, 1910

The spirit that prevails is this: in all scientific studies Darwinian evolution is taught, often anti-theistically, and seldom is any attempt made to harmonize it with the early part of Genesis, for example. Ussher's chronology is still the cause of trouble, in the light of geology, etc. But these are the least serious issues. Much more serious is the general agnostic atmosphere pervading everything and deadening all convictions, those as to sin and truth included. In line with this, a broad spirit of tolerance is insisted upon, especially in matters of religion, and any and all are branded as narrow who dare think otherwise. That word "narrow" is one of Satan's deadliest weapons, it seems to me; for most people would apparently rather be shot than be called narrow. Thus it is even as Christ predicted—the broad way to destruction is thronged, but few are climbing the narrow way that leads to life.

When we come to distinctively Christian and religious matters, the situation is even worse. "Practically everyone" believes that the Bible is full of contradictions and errors, etc., etc. Even earnest Christians seem to feel that it doesn't matter. The New Testament fares little better than the Old at the hands of critics, and the supernatural is expunged from both. And against all this scarcely a voice of any authority is raised in protest, from within the ranks. In the women's colleges things are even worse, as I know from my sister who was at Vassar and from a recent conversation with one of the Y.W.C.A. secretaries, who is firm in the faith and alive to the situation.

In spite of everything the work of the Y.M.C.A. goes on, men are really won to Christ, and many good workers are sent into active Christian service. But it is *in spite* of all this.

Now the leaders, I feel, do not all of them by any means see the real tendency of this modern teaching, especially of the Biblical teaching, which in the name of Christianity really discredits Christ and the Christian faith. Either they do not clearly see the issues, or if they do, they seek to compromise. This is evident from the kind of speakers approved of, and still more so from the Bible teachers and teaching that are popular. There is tremendous zeal and energy among many students and leaders here, and my only desire is that they should find the truth. Dr. Zwemer sees all these things clearly and has helped a lot, but now he is going, and as far as I know there is no one with a theological training (which is almost essential, to enable one to see the real issues) who can take his place and help to keep the student movement pure, strong and evangelical. The need is tremendous and the opportunity immense. I should like nothing better than to get into the fight, right here in the American colleges, should the Lord close my way to the foreign field.

One other word I would like to add. The teaching about the kingdom of God is entirely with the idea that it is gradually to be brought in by our making the world better. This of course fits in with the socialistic ideas of the day, but hardly with Scripture! And here again, in the college world scarcely a voice is raised in support of God's Word.

I do hope you will come and help. I feel sure it would mean a better quality of work here, and a greater number of really equipped men for the work abroad. And I would like to add a word about the China Inland Mission, which I am only beginning really to know and with which you doubtless are better acquainted. What I want to say is that if you join yourself with them in some capacity, you will have a praying constituency behind you such as no other organization I know of would afford.

12

A HEART TESTED

1910–1912

AGE 23–24

And evermore beside him on his way
The unseen Christ shall move,
That he may lean upon His arm and say,
"Dost Thou, dear Lord, approve?"

—H. W. Longfellow

It was the summer of 1910. Borden was leaving for Europe to attend the Edinburgh Conference, and on the steamer, amid all the bustle of departure, was engrossed in conversation with a friend whose acquaintance he had recently made.

"I want to help you in the work you are doing," he said quietly, "and will send you a hundred dollars a month for the next year. If you will come to my cabin, I will write the first check now."

"We went down," Mr. Don O. Shelton recalled when that friendship had become one of the most precious in his life, "and he wrote the check and gave it to me. When I reached home I found it was for two hundred dollars. *He is going abroad,* I thought, *and has made it for two months this time.* But exactly one month later came another check for two hundred dollars, and again the following month, two hundred.

He is giving it all in six months, was my conclusion. But when he returned at the end of the summer he continued to send two hundred dollars a month through the entire year.

"I was learning to know Will Borden, one of whose characteristics it was always to do better than he promised, more and not less than he led you to expect."

Needless to say, this was when he felt his confidence to be well-founded, as in the case of The National Bible Institute under the leadership of Mr. Shelton.

Twenty years of work in the Y.M.C.A. and in Bible Conferences had convinced this earnest evangelist that something new and different in the way of approach was needed if the multitudes who never darken a church door were to hear the Gospel. He had given up a promising career for no other reason than that he realized the Christian man's responsibility for a situation such as we have around us today. More than half the people in the United States, as he well knew, were outside the membership of any church. Seventy-five percent of the young men were bowing down to gods of wealth, lust, and pleasure, and were worshiping them alone.

"Of what value is it preaching to empty seats," he questioned, "when the people who ought to occupy them are in crowded tenements or on street corners or in the parks, and do not hear the faintest whisper of the message?"

The outcome, after much prayer and consideration, was a simple, earnest effort, on the part of businessmen chiefly, to reach the crowds in the city of New York. It was on a June day in 1907 that the first meeting was held at the busy hour of noon. A low platform under a tree in Madison Square Garden was all he used, with a little organ and a group of singers to lead familiar hymns. The speakers were businessmen, the language was that of the newspaper rather than the theological hall. But the results were amazing. It was no unusual thing to see three hundred men listening with riveted attention through the daily half hour, and very soon other noon meetings had to be started—and a school for lay evangelists to meet the need of training for such work.

"The people hear the gospel gladly," Mr. Shelton was writing a few weeks later. "In Madison Square Garden more men have assembled daily to hear the message than gather on Sundays for any Protestant church service in Greater New York, with two or three exceptions. And what representative throngs we have! Working-men from nearby buildings, clerks from offices, boot-blacks sitting on their kits, street cleaners, messenger boys, police officers, contractors, well-to-do business men, drunkards, the unemployed and discouraged, editors and professional people, all listening with the same interest. The attention is so close at times as to be pathetic. . . . The gospel is still the most winsome message in the world.

"We never take up a collection. The one object is to reach men, and from the beginning we have had crowds of them. The work thus far has resulted in many transformations of character. Some of those who have been greatly helped have expressed their purpose to unite with churches at once. We believe that we are carrying out Christ's idea in going to the people and not waiting for them to come to us."

All this interested Borden deeply, and further acquaintance with the work only increased his sense of its value, so that when he was asked in the fall of 1910 to become one of the directors of the National Bible Institute, it was a call he could not refuse. The position was no sinecure. It involved frequent journeys to New York to attend the board meetings, and the problems of the work called for much thought and prayer. A large part of his vacation in the summer of 1911 was spent in the heat and hurry of New York, taking a full share in meetings and other activities. Of this Mr. Shelton writes:

> I find in my diary under date of May 8, 1911, the following sentences: "Mr. William W. Borden came up from Princeton today to cooperate for a few weeks in the work of the National Bible Institute. A noble, generous, Christ-like young man— a rare gift of God to the work under his care!"

> We placed a desk for him in my own office, and he continually manifested an eager desire to enter into the work in every possible way. Responsibility for our four gospel halls was delegated to him, and he kept in close touch with the superintendents, counseling with them in regard to all the details. He investigated men who were being considered for

positions of trust. He gave much thought and prayer to drafting the "Principles and Practice" of the National Bible Institute, and prepared a document which has been of exceeding great value in its development. . . .

It is a joy to recall his first appearance at our Madison Square meeting in the open air. His address was brief, but remarkably vigorous and direct. He stood there as a witness to the saving power of Jesus Christ. As he spoke, I rejoiced that the large company of listeners had before them one of the manliest, purest and noblest of our Lord's modern witnesses. His radiant face, unaffected manner, and joyous, fervent testimony to the power of the Christian faith made the occasion memorable. . . .

As a member of the Board of Directors he was a valued counselor. He turned the white light of Scripture on every matter that came up for consideration. His presence in any meeting was a moral and spiritual tonic.

All his work began, continued and ended in prayer. Again and again, at our office, he would suggest before taking up the consideration of any important matter that we should unite in waiting upon God. Prayer was to him the first means to be used in accomplishing any object. And how simple, direct, unselfish and childlike his prayers were! He prayed as one confident that his heavenly Father would hear and answer.

That he was thinking deeply about the work of the National Bible Institute was evident from the fact that he had arranged, before coming to New York, for a visit that he thought would be helpful from a representative of the China Inland Mission. "Owe no man anything, but to love one another," was a scriptural injunction that was authoritative with him, and he wanted the practical methods explained by which a mission with a thousand foreign and four thousand national workers was able to carry it out. With an intimate knowledge of the bookkeeping of the mission, Miss Mary Brayton, the head of its accounting department in Philadelphia, had consented to make the matter plain, and it was an interesting hour in the New York office as it was all talked over in detail.

By never making a purchase, large or small, until there was money in hand to pay for it, the visitor explained, and by carefully estimating running expenses and putting aside a daily proportion of the income, whatever it might be, to meet them, there were always funds in hand for coming charges.

> One cannot be running out every day to pay one's gas bill! But we can and do put aside a dollar and a half a day, or whatever the proportion may be, towards it. We do the same for our rent, fuel, electric light, taxes on property and all other running expenses, so that the money is there when it is needed. We paid the rent on Saturday, for example, but on Monday we begin just the same putting away for the next month or quarter. And these funds are rarely drawn upon for any other purpose. We reckon that we have spent that money already. And as to other things, we never give an order unless we have actual cash in hand to meet it. We do not draw upon probabilities.

"If the China Inland Mission can do it, never making an appeal for funds nor taking a collection," Borden exclaimed, "surely we can, by prayer and watchfulness! And I do think we ought not to buy even a broom until we have money in hand to pay for it."

But it was not only in these ways he sought to be of use. The work was growing fast and it was hard to keep pace with its requirements. Permanent offices were badly needed, and some places in which the students could meet for their classes. A hall also was required for the old Jerry McAuley Mission, which had passed into Mr. Shelton's care.

The neighborhood in which they hoped to locate was a desperate one, almost every corner for many blocks in all directions being occupied by saloons or dance-halls, with a plentiful sprinkling of movie theaters. Thousands of young people thronged the streets at night and there were few places open to them in which the influences were not harmful.

The time had come for action, so Borden set to work under Mr. Shelton's direction to make the needs and opportunities known and to gather a circle of praying friends. Together they investigated every street in that section of "the tenderloin," and made a map showing exactly what there was and was not—a map which was in itself the most powerful of appeals. The circular Borden sent out, signed with his own name as chairman of the building committee, contained the map in full, dotted over with more than three hundred hell-traps of various sorts and the plea for the activities of the National Bible Institute where it was so much needed "as a protest against iniquity and for the reaching of the sin-sick and for the protection of the innocent."

More important still was his work that summer in forming the "Circle of Intercession." This was his own idea, born of his conviction that prayer is fundamental and not secondary in work for God. Buildings might be put up and organization developed, but unless prayer kept pace with these activities all would be in vain. So it was for prayer Borden appealed most earnestly of all.

"Our Circle of Intercession has become most dear to us," Mrs. Shelton wrote when the efforts had been rewarded, "for we realize that it was through Mr. Borden's consecrated energy and perseverance that it was formed two years ago. That was a wonderful summer for us—Mr. Borden gave so much time and thought in Mr. Shelton's office to the work; and for me there stands out vividly the morning when he most feelingly expressed his sympathy because of a dreaded ordeal before me. Every contact with him revealed the depths of a wonderful Christian character."

Back for his last year at Princeton, Borden was harder at work than ever, preparing a course of lectures he was to deliver to the students of the National Bible Institute. The Epistle to the Galatians was his subject, and the long list of books he consulted shows how thorough was his preparation. Luther's commentary he enjoyed especially, but it was only one of several. How he could possibly make time in the midst of his third year in seminary to complete and deliver these seven lectures is a mystery. Week by week his class in the marble Collegiate Church numbered from sixty to a hundred.

"His handling of this difficult Epistle showed that he had completely mastered his material," was Mr. Shelton's comment. "His outlines were clear and comprehensive, and he made the book a living message to the hearers."

Early in 1912 the National Bible Institute was passing

through a time of difficult trial. In spite of the directors' efforts to keep clear of debt, a deficit of five thousand dollars had accumulated. There was much prayer about it, and an earnest desire to learn from past experience. But how was the deficit to be wiped out?

A meeting of the board was called, for it looked as though there would have to be serious retrenchment. Borden had come up from Princeton. His financial contributions to the work were considerable, and no one was looking to him to do more. The morning had passed in earnest conference and prayer.

"I must make the 2:04 train," he said at length, "and shall have to run for it."

He was writing on a slip of paper as he spoke, and pushing it across the table to the treasurer, Mr. Hugh Monro, he made for the door. It was a check for five thousand two hundred dollars! Without a word he had taken up the entire indebtedness. It was not only the gift, but the way in which it was done that was so like him! Nobody dreamed he was writing a check, and before they realized it he was gone.

But he gave more than money. A few weeks later he was in the throes of his final examinations at Princeton. The mountains were calling him. After a heavy winter's work he was eager for a few weeks in Switzerland among the glaciers he loved. His passage was taken and everything was ready when it came to his knowledge that Mr. Shelton was on the verge of a breakdown. Calling at his office, Borden found that the doctor had ordered him to take complete rest. The need for it was urgent, but there seemed no one to take his place.

"Looks as though I might have to change my plans a bit, and help," was the entry in Borden's journal for that day.

Quietly then his passage was given up and the trip postponed. He was sufficiently familiar with the National Bible Institute to step in effectively, and before long was fully in charge. This meant that he was responsible not only for the office work. There were the daily open-air meetings, the oversight of the students in their classes and practical training, the charge of four rescue missions and of the monthly magazine, as well as the financial care of all this work.

It was a serious undertaking, the more so as Borden had decided before entering upon it that he must not be his own Providence in the matter of supplies. Mr. Shelton was not himself in a position to finance the work, and when sufficient means were not forthcoming he and his helpers had no resource but prayer. To strengthen them in their attitude of looking to the Lord in faith had long been Borden's desire. He believed that the promises of God were absolutely true and dependable. Here then was an opportunity for proving the reality of his own faith as well as strengthening that of his fellow-workers. He would continue to give just as he had been giving, but would not permit himself to escape difficulties by the easy method of drawing upon his own bank account. And this led to a remarkable experience, as Mrs. Shelton writes:

> There followed a time of severe testing along financial lines for the young substitute. Days passed without a dollar coming in—and mission superintendents and others needing their salaries! Some time before, Mr. Borden had faced the question of making up known deficiencies in the various Christian enterprises in which he was interested, and as his gifts were always thoughtfully and prayerfully given he had decided against it. Yet here was a temptation! How much easier to put his hand in his pocket and make up this lack than to spend hours in prayer alone and with friends, awaiting God's gracious answer. But the answers came—and with them such a sense of the reality and nearness of the living God as days and hours of ease could never have afforded.

It was the hottest summer that had been known in New York for many years, and the Bordens had just moved from Princeton to a house on Fifty-fifth Street for the time being. It was convenient to be nearer the office, but the heat of the city was overpowering. In spite of this, Mrs. Borden went with her son to some of the noonday meetings and put off her sailing for Europe until he could come. But that was weeks ahead and meanwhile the pressure of the work was heavy.

"Gee," William exclaimed in the office one day, "if I had known what I was coming up against, I doubt whether I would have made this suggestion!"

Yet in addition to all his other occupations he was caring for an invalid uncle that summer. He made time to go frequently to Long Beach, where his relatives were staying, to be a cheer to his aunt and to wheel his uncle up and down the boardwalk in a chair, returning to the city by an early train in the morning.

"The Price of Power" was the title of an article he was writing at Long Beach one Sunday for the paper that Mr. Shelton edited. It was the outgrowth of a thought that had long been in his mind. A saying quoted by Mr. Moody had deeply impressed him: "The world has yet to see what God can do with a fully consecrated man." To be such a man was his highest ambition, and he was learning how real and practical is the price that has to be paid. He was learning that it comes into everything, and that it may be expressed in the one inclusive word, obedience. Obedience toward God had come to be the keynote of his life—instant, glad obedience. To him, the Word of God was final.

"On the other hand—" some of us are tempted to say. To him there was no "other hand."

If he saw that in anything his life did not square with the Word of God, that ended it. The secret of power, he had learned, was that secret open to all—"the Holy Spirit whom God hath given *to them that obey Him*" (Acts 5:32). He was speaking from experience when he wrote:

> There must be a definite determination to do God's will—a will to obey. Christ laid down the conditions of discipleship as denying self and following Him, and that is just what is required here. Each one must examine his life and put away all sin, not holding on to anything which the Spirit tells him he should let go.
>
> One of the hardest things anyone can have to do is to confess he has wronged another. But we read, "If thou bring thy gift to the altar, and there rememberest that thy brother hath aught against thee, leave there thy gift before the altar, and go thy way; first be reconciled to thy brother, and then come and offer thy gift."[1] We touch upon this matter of confession to others because it has played such a prominent

---
[1] Matthew 5:23–24

part in spiritual awakenings, and because of the conviction
that lack of such confession is the cause of much powerless-
ness in Christian service.

Questions of life-work also need to be met squarely and
the inquiry honestly made: "Lord, what wilt Thou have me
to do?" The answer may not come at once, but there should
be a willingness and determination to do His will, whatever
service it may involve, at home or abroad. These are but
suggestions to indicate what is involved in absolute consecration to Christ, which is so necessary to real obedience. Do
you lack power? Ask yourself, *Have I ever fully surrendered?
Have I definitely consecrated myself, put myself at God's dis-
posal, to use as He deems best?*

It must be admitted, however, that there are those who at
some time of vision or conflict have won a victory and taken
this great step, and yet have not subsequently had real power
in their lives. What is the reason? Cases differ, but may we
not say that it was probably through failure to make this principle of complete obedience permanent in their lives? Christ's
rule for discipleship as given in Matthew 16:24 has been referred to above. Do you know how it reads in Luke, and what
the additional feature is which has there been preserved for
us? It is just one word: "If any man would come after me, let
him deny himself and take up his cross *daily* and follow me."
Daily—that is the thing to note. It is not enough to take up
the cross once and then lay it down when the burden grows
wearisome.

The need for daily application of this principle appears in
two ways: first, old questions which have been faced and
downed as we thought, will come up again; and secondly,
there will arise new problems which were not covered by the
original act of consecration. Many who have faced the question of life-work, and decided for the foreign field, illustrate
this. It was at tremendous cost they made the decision, and
possibly there was the thought that afterwards all would be
plain sailing. But no: the same old problems had to be fought
out, and there were new ones too to face. The principle of
Christ's supremacy could not be lost sight of for a moment.
Satan, when defeated, left Christ but for a little season. How
much less, when he has been ousted from our lives at some
conference or on some mountain-top, will he despair of finding a foothold when we are on the plain of everyday living

again. Obedience, which is the price of power, must not only be absolute but daily. Are we paying this part of the price?

It may be there are others who have consecrated themselves to Christ and do not seek to make this a daily attitude of life, and yet fail to receive real power. Where this is the case, may it not be due to imperfect application of the principle of obedience? It is comparatively easy to isolate the great issues, the big problems, and to deal with them by the grace of God. But there are many so-called "little things" which are apt to be overlooked. These grieve and quench the Spirit in no less real a way than the others.[2] They are difficult to deal with, and many Christians do not seem to recognize what they are at all—though ignorance does not save us from the consequences in this any more than in other spheres. We must study the Word of God, daily see ourselves in that glass, asking God to search us and know our hearts, try us and know our thoughts, and see if there be any wicked way in us.

Mr. Speer in his *Principles of Jesus* has indicated four great guiding principles that our Lord laid down—namely, purity, honesty, unselfishness and love. These are simple and plain enough; yet how many of us are checking up our every thought and word and deed by these? How many of us are asking in everything, *Is this pleasing to Him?* Our personal habits, our amusements, all our interactions with others, business or social, should be considered in this light. We must seek not merely to avoid quenching the Spirit; we must be careful lest we grieve Him.

Obedience, absolute and unqualified, which is made a daily principle of living, carried even into little things, this is the price of power.

Of course there must not be a selfish motive, and we must not fail to ask in definite believing prayer for the Holy Spirit. But if the conditions are met, God will make good His promise, "Ye shall receive power." How the power will manifest itself in our lives need not concern us here. The saying still holds good—"The world has yet to see what God can do with a fully consecrated man." Only as filled with His Spirit can

---

[2]"Self-pleasing in little things brings darkness. The lightest cloud before the sun will prevent it from focusing its rays to a burning point through the convex glass. Spiritually, the result is the same even with small, thin, scarcely visible acts of self-will."—Alexander Maclaren, D.D.

we hope to win men from darkness to light and to faith in Christ. Shall we not each one resolve, from henceforth, to obey Him absolutely in all things, small and great?

Reality was what gave his words their power. Before Mr. Shelton's return to the office Borden was tested, himself, in the matter of putting duty before pleasure. The first reunion of his class at Yale had come and he managed to get away for the weekend. But the triennial banquet, the climax of the proceedings, did not come until Monday, and there was a Board meeting of the National Bible Institute that day that he felt he should attend. Great was the consternation of his classmates when it appeared that he was leaving before the banquet. Many old friends were there, among them his roommate, Mac Vilas.

"Indeed you won't go to New York," they exclaimed with insistence. "We won't let you go!"

"But we might as well have talked to the Rock of Gibraltar," Mac remarked.

Borden managed to return the following day, and that he entered fully into the spirit of the occasion may be seen from the note in his journal: "Attended to a few things at the office and left for New Haven, getting to the field for the game, which Yale won from Harvard, 9–6. Our class wore farmers' costumes. It was a great jollification!"

The summer had taken more out of the young substitute than he realized, but even on the voyage to Europe for a much-curtailed holiday he was working at an important task. The Moody Bible Institute of Chicago, of which he was a director, thought it timely to prepare a statement setting forth its doctrinal standards. Borden was on the committee appointed for that purpose. His application papers to the China Inland Mission had already called for such a statement, and he had with him the *Doctrinal Basis of the National Bible Institute*, covering the same ground, a document which had been largely his work. This he enclosed with his letter to Chicago, concerning which Dr. Gray wrote to Mrs. Borden: "The letter is much valued by me, and I trust that when the biographer has finished with it, it may be returned to my hands."

Kronprinz Wilhelm
July 21, 1912

Dear Dr. Gray,

In accordance with your wishes I am taking this opportunity to draw up my suggestions for the proposed doctrinal basis of the Moody Institute.

First:

The purpose. As I understand it, the need is for a statement embodying what we feel is essential to sound doctrine in the teaching and work of the Institute. This statement should be an aid to the trustees, not only as a standard for checking up the teaching staff, but also to guide them in the selection of new trustees at any time—written assent to the doctrinal basis being required of all present and future members of the Board of Trustees as well as the teaching staff, and also a pledge to give notice of any future change of opinion, and willingness to resign if requested to do so.

Second:

What is the essential to sound doctrine? I feel that the inspiration and authority of Scripture; God: His being and attributes; Christ: His person (Deity) and work (atonement); the Holy Spirit: His person and work; man's sinful state and need of regeneration; the way of salvation from the guilt of sin (justification by faith alone) and from the power of sin (sanctification); the return of Christ and future rewards and punishments are the essentials.

Third

The order and phrasing of the statement. I would say at once that I do not feel that it will be possible to employ Scripture language only, both from the nature and extent of the ground to be covered and the exigencies of the present day with its requirement of great exactness. We should, however, seek to be as brief as may be consistent with clearness. Coming then to the actual phrasing, I would suggest the following:

DOCTRINAL BASIS OF THE MOODY BIBLE INSTITUTE

We believe in the inspiration, integrity, and authority of the Bible. By this is meant a miraculous guiding work of the Holy Spirit in their original writing, extending to all parts of the Scriptures equally, applying even to the choice of words. Moreover, it is our conviction that God has exercised such singular care and providence through the ages in preserving the written word, that the Scriptures as we now have them are in every essential particular as originally given, so that the result is the very word of God, the only infallible rule of faith and practice, containing all things necessary to salvation and sound doctrine.

We believe in the deity of our Lord Jesus Christ and His death on the cross as a true substitute, and that His death was a sufficient expiation for the guilt of all men.

We believe in the Holy Spirit as a Divine person, distinct from the Father and the Son, who convicts the world of sin, regenerates and dwells in the true believer, quickening and empowering him in all his life and service.

We believe that all men are by nature sinful and unable to save themselves, and that "except a man be born again, he cannot see the kingdom of God."

We believe that men are justified by faith (in Jesus Christ) alone and are accounted righteous before God only for the merit of our Lord and Savior Jesus Christ.

We believe that sanctification is a work of God's free grace whereby, being renewed in the whole man, we are enabled more and more to die unto sin and to live unto righteousness.

We believe in the second coming of our Lord, as a personal, visible and glorious advent on this earth.

We believe in the everlasting conscious blessedness of the saved and in the everlasting conscious punishment of the lost.

As a conclusion I would suggest an adaptation of the paragraph in the Moody Church statement to the effect that while specifying these doctrines, we by no means undervalue or set aside any Scriptures of the Old or New Testaments.

Of course I do not pretend that this is final, but it embodies my thoughts for the present. I hope you can read it all. Kindly keep the enclosed typewritten statement with this letter (of which I have no copy by the way) as I would like to refer to the two together in Chicago when we meet next fall, God willing.

Sincerely yours,
William W. Borden

"So often nowadays we are told that it does not matter what men think, it only matters what they do," wrote a friend of Borden's from Bryn Mawr College. "It is a striking contrast to turn back to the Gospels and find the Lord Himself reversing this emphasis. His great question was, 'What think ye of Christ?' 'Who do men say that I am?'

"This Bill realized fully. He knew that it mattered supremely what he thought. He was a great help to me always in the Christian life, and I wish that more might know of his devotion to Christ. I wish that people who say it doesn't matter what you believe could only see how much it mattered to him, and the results those very beliefs produced in his life."

13

A SOUL BENT TO OBEY

1912

Age 24

The Master said, "Come, follow"—
That was all.
Earth's joys grew dim,
My soul went after Him;
I rose and followed—
That was all.
Will you not follow if you hear His call?

—Selected

Commencement exercises coincided with the centennial celebrations of Princeton Seminary, making Borden's graduation especially memorable that year. From all over the world came congratulatory messages for Princeton—the oldest seminary of the Presbyterian Church in America. She had graduated almost six thousand students, over four hundred of whom had gone abroad as missionaries. Many distinguished visitors were there for the occasion and the Borden home had many guests.

"President Patton was at his best," William wrote, "and preached a tremendous sermon on 'The faith once for all delivered to the saints.'"

Dr. Speer's missionary address was equally inspiring. After recalling the devoted lives of Princeton graduates in many a field, he continued:

> We owe it to the fathers who went before us to stand afraid at no opportunity and flinch at no call. They taught us the glory of unswerving fidelity. The men who have gone out from these halls have always known the duty of staying by duty until the sun went down. They were taught that God is patient and that His servants need not be anxious or afraid. The Seminary has always sought to breed in her sons a dauntless and unfearing supernaturalism. The missionary enterprise is too vast for a mere human will to sustain. Its difficulties, its necessities, its problems, its ideals call for God. Its sufficiency is in Him alone. Here, men learned that God was in the Beginning and that God stands back of the end. With God and for God such men have dared all things, and have not fainted nor grown weary.

In the midst of the celebrations came the granting of diplomas to the graduating students. In his Line-A-Day journal, Borden noted:

May 6, 1912

> Got our diplomas in Alexandria Hall. The academic procession was quite brilliant. Four fine addresses in the afternoon. Speer's was best, on Princeton in the Mission Field.

Little more than six months remained for Borden of life in his own land, and his activities were full and far-reaching. "He fulfilled a great time in a short time," Keith Falconer said. He was running a race, his eye was on the goal.

The day after he had taken his last examination at Princeton, for example, he traveled to New York to see Dr. John R. Mott to formulate plans for the work he was to take up in the fall in connection with the Student Volunteer Movement. A three months' schedule had been made out for visits to various colleges. He was to speak especially on the needs of the Muslim world, before sailing for Egypt on his way to China. It was felt that a few months at Cairo at the language school, would be advantageous, not only for the study of Arabic and the Koran,

but of Islam generally before attempting to meet it in its strong-
holds in western China.

Released from his responsibilities in Mr. Shelton's office,
Borden had spent a few weeks in Switzerland, climbing the
Jungfrau and the Wetterhorn, and had returned to New York
refreshed for his work in the colleges. Then came his ordination, which took place in the Moody Church, Chicago, as its
elders recorded:

> He was one of our boys. This was the church of his child-
> hood. . . . Here he returned for ordination after completing
> his Seminary course, and as we examined him in view of that
> step his testimony rang true as steel to every cardinal doctrine
> of Holy Writ.
>
> On September 9, 1912, we set him apart to the ministry
> of our Lord and Savior Jesus Christ in a foreign land, little
> thinking that his ministry was to be to our Lord himself in the
> better land.

The service was simple but impressive, marked by contrasts
that gave the daily papers a good deal to say at the time. That
a man of his age and prospects should turn away from all the
world could offer and devote himself to a life of loneliness and
hardship in a remote province in China, "the darkest and mean-
est section of the Orient," as one paper seriously said, was
beyond the understanding of many. But another Chicago daily
gave an account of the proceedings that must have arrested
attention, printing in full on its front page the hymn that seemed
to sum up all there was to be said:

> When I survey the wondrous cross
> On which the Prince of Glory died,
> My richest gain I count but loss
> And pour contempt on all my pride.
>
> Were the whole realm of nature mine,
> That were an offering far too small;
> Love so amazing, so divine,
> Demands my life, my soul, my all.

Borden did not see the papers. That side of the matter was
painful to him. In a circular letter to twelve Princeton classmates who kept up a correspondence, he mentioned the fact of

his ordination, by writing: "I am sorry there was such unnecessary publicity, and hope you fellows will discount what was said very liberally."

The real impressive quality of the service lay in the love and compassion of the great assembly for one who had grown up among them, whose consecration to Christ they knew full well; in the sermon by Dr. James Gray, dean of the Bible Institute, and the charge given by Dr. John Timothy Stone, Pastor of the Fourth Presbyterian Church, and in the prayers with which Borden was committed to the Lord, on the very spot from which Moody had so often preached, as the ministers and elders gathered round him:

> We set him apart for the work to which he was called. The hands of the lowly were laid upon his head. The Holy Spirit filled him. The grace of the Omnipotent was in his life.

That grace was very real in his mother's experience as well, in the hour which was to her the climax of her sacrifice. From his childhood she had consecrated him to the Lord, and his call to missionary work had come as an answer to her many prayers. Yet, since his father's death, she had learned to lean upon him in everything, and the very thought of separation seemed at times unbearable. Firm as a rock, there had been no wavering in his purpose. He knew as well as she did that her deepest desire was one with his own. They stood together, and his strength had helped her no less than his tenderness. But the separation had until this time been prospective. Now it was coming near. His ordination meant, as Mrs. Borden realized, that they were committed to the sacrifice that seemed as if it must cost her very life.

And then—there is no explaining it apart from the presence of the Lord himself—as in that hour she held back nothing, a wonderful peace filled her heart. Physical weakness, even, was replaced by strength, so that she was able to meet all the demands of the dreaded situation when it came, with gladness. For there is a fellowship with Christ that infinitely compensates any cost at which it is won.

To a friend who about this time expressed surprise that he was "throwing himself away as a missionary," Borden replied,

"*You* have not seen heathenism."

He had; and the constraining love of Christ made him, as one of his Princeton classmates put it, "a missionary, first, last and all the time."

"No one would have known from Borden's life and talk that he was a millionaire," wrote another, "but no one could have helped knowing that he was a Christian and alive for missions."

Yet, to him, souls were just as precious in America as across the ocean, and his responsibility as great for all whom he could reach. His friend, Mr. Hugh Monro, treasurer of the National Bible Institute, said in this connection:

> Not a few of us, under the influence of evangelistic services, or some other spiritual tonic, are filled with zeal for the salvation of others. At certain seasons, when we have given ourselves specially to prayer, perhaps, and the study of God's Word, we are awakened to a new concern about the spiritual welfare of those around us. But there was nothing spasmodic about Borden's zeal. He had that unique thing, an abiding passion for the souls of men. It was his constant thought; it seemed never absent from his mind.
>
> Most of us look for occasions which may afford a suitable opportunity for soul-winning, and excuse our lack of devotion and diligence because we feel that such an opportunity is not present. We continually hesitate to broach the subject of another's salvation, lest the occasion should not be favorable. Yet Borden found such opportunities continually.

Visiting with his mother, for example, in the home of some relatives, he became concerned about the butler, who was drinking heavily. At dinner one evening, when not sober, the butler let some ice cream slip off a plate, almost ruining a Worth gown. Learning that he had been dismissed, Mrs. Borden mentioned the matter to William. It was not their responsibility, maybe, but the following Sunday his mother's maid, walking in the direction of the butler's house, heard quick steps behind her and found William at her side.

"Melanie," he said, "I am going to inquire for the butler. Couldn't we have prayer together that God will speak to him today?"

"So we stopped right there on the street," the maid recalled. "Then Mr. William went on to the house, and the butler truly turned to the Lord that day. A fortnight later, he took pneumonia and died."

Did Borden regret the effort he had made to see him?

It was not easy in his busy life to make time for correspondence, but he could not have regretted the letters he wrote, at some sacrifice, to a poor fellow in jail, apparently a stranger to him. The prisoner replied:

> I think of you a great deal, and I am more than thankful for what you have done for me. I have had a hard time getting back to faith, but with your help and the help of God I can call myself a Christian again. . . . I have received a letter from my wife saying that you have sent her a copy of St. John's Gospel. She is very thankful to you for it, also for what you have done for me. You cannot imagine how much the brute I feel when I think of having done what I have—leaving my wife and baby, to be locked up in a felon's cell. . . . I hope with the help of God that henceforth I will be a better man.

The real test of fitness for missionary work abroad is not so much a high educational standard as the faith and love, the prayer and devotedness, that win men at home.

Borden's message in the colleges was of the sort to appeal to a strong type of personality. Great knowledge had but deepened his conviction that the two hundred million Muslims were by far the hardest as well as the most neglected field for missionary enterprise. The very difficulties attracted him.

Kansu, for example—that lonely, far-off province in northwest China, with its three million Muslims among a hardy population of Mongols, Tibetans and Chinese—was the sphere in which he hoped to labor. Peking was much more central, strategic, some would have said. There were many mosques in the capital, and a post as organizing secretary for work among Muslims throughout China could easily have been arranged. But Borden was looking for a harder assignment. Just because Kansu was isolated, thrust out between Mongolia and Tibet, because the missionaries were few and the work difficult, because the people he longed to reach were there in multitudes, and no one was set apart for work among them, Kansu was the place of his choice.

Ho-chow was there with its bigoted, proud race of Muslims, Arabs by descent. There, too, were the Tung-hsiang, remnants of the old Hun tribes in the mountains, long since converted to Islam at the point of the sword. And there were the Salas from distant Samarkand, with their Turkish speech and faces, Muslim exiles who had tramped across central Asia hundreds of years ago to find a home beside the Yellow River. And these virile, dominating sons of Islam were mingled in the western part of the province with Tibetans from the border-marches and Mongols from north of the Great Wall. More than this, the Great Road running through the province—itself a thousand miles from east to west—led on across the Gobi Desert to the Muslim heart of Central Asia, linking up city after city in which no missionary had ever labored, and giving access to the mingled peoples of that vast region, one of the most neglected, from the missionary point of view, in the world. That waiting heart of Asia, how it appealed to him, just because so few were willing to lay down their lives that these, too, might have the message of Redeeming Love!

A handful of brave men and women were there, representing the two missions working in the province, and forty days' journey westward, two lonely pioneers, almost as far from the nearest missionaries on the other side.[1] More than sixty cities in Kansu itself without a witness for Christ; four-fifths of its population still unreached; three million Muslims for whom no one could be spared because the inadequate staff was absorbed in work among the Chinese. There was no doctor, no hospital in the entire province, and those vast lands beyond with mil-

---

[1]The China Inland Mission and the Christian and Missionary Alliance were the only missions working in Kansu at that time. The solitary outpost in Central Asia is the city of Ti-hwa-fu, in which Mr. George Hunter and Mr. P.C. Mather of the China Inland Mission were still working alone in 1926.

lions more for whom there were so few to care—that was the sphere that is waiting still.[2]

With a background of such thoughts and purposes, Borden brought to his work in the colleges a reality that could not but be felt. The joy and inspiration of a great task possessed him, and he could not speak of missionary work, even in its hardest phases, as sacrifice. To him it was privilege of the highest order, the privilege that comes not to angels but to men, and to us once only, now, in this fleeting life.

Two books were his traveling companions at this time, and give some idea as to his talks in the colleges—one, the mission-study book for the year, Dr. Zwemer's *Unoccupied Mission Fields of Africa and Asia*, full of facts that were the strongest arguments, and the other *The Threefold Secret of the Spirit*, so worn and marked as to tell its own story. It went everywhere with him and its truths were being wrought into his deepest life. Divided into three parts, it deals first with the secret of the incoming of the Holy Spirit; then with the secret of His fullness; and lastly with the secret of His constant manifestation in our lives. Borden's copy was marked in the way he had with all his best-loved books, one sentence stood out as meaning much to him:

The supreme human condition of the fullness of the Spirit is a life wholly surrendered to God to do His will.

Nothing greater or more glorious could be desired, and Borden knew of nothing that brought deeper satisfaction. Life was not, to him a question of being or having this or that, it was simply a question of the will of God—knowing it, doing it, loving it. And such a life, he knew, was possible even in college, through the indwelling of the Holy Spirit. So his message was one of gladness and power.

Beginning at Schenectady, New York, in September, he managed to visit thirty colleges and seminaries before sailing

---

[2]More complete information about this most interesting province can be obtained from two books written on the spot, publications of the China Inland Mission: *The Call of China's Great North-West* by Mrs. Howard Taylor and *Despatches from North-West China* by Miss Mildred Cable and Miss Francesca French.

for Egypt in December. One to three days in a place gave opportunity for interviews as well as meetings, and his time was so filled that it was with difficulty he got away on his twenty-fifth birthday to spend the evening with his mother.

In many interviews, Mr. Robert Wilder's question often came to his mind, and with the background of sea experience, he would ask, "Are you steering or drifting?"

The question served to open up the subject of a student's choices in life. The danger of drifting was manifest. If a man said he was steering, it was easy to go on: "What is your goal, and Who is with you on board?"

To cut out indecision was what Borden urged. In a Greek New Testament given to a friend he had written: "If any man wills to do His will, he shall know. . ." (John 7:17).

"It was a favorite passage of his," wrote the classmate, "and one upon which his own Christian activities were built up. Like his Master, he realized that it was nearly always a question of whether a man wanted to or not. Bill always referred the matter back to the will. In talking about a Bible group which was failing, the leader having grown lax, I remember Bill's saying that it might have been the best group in our class if the leader had been willing to pay the price."

The uttermost for the utmost was the price as he saw it— the uttermost of surrender on our part for the utmost of what God will do in and through us. It was a high ideal. Often Borden would meet one to whom it seemed too high with another question: "Are you willing to be made willing?"

"I remember that to some of us this directness of appeal seemed at times to lack sympathy with the other person's point of view," continued his friend. "But it was the sort of thing to draw out the best that was in a man, and gathered to itself those who were willing."

One thing evident to all was that the speaker himself was paying the price and finding it a wonderful exchange. And this gave force to the missionary side of his message, which consisted chiefly in a clear presentation of facts. For Borden felt with Dr. Zwemer that we do not need to plead the cause of missions. The case is there. All we ask is a verdict.

"If ten men are carrying a log," he said, at Andover, "nine of them on the little end and one at the heavy end, and you wanted to help, which end would you lift on?"[3]

Difficulties he spoke of as a challenge to faith and consecration, and while not minimizing them, especially in presenting the situation in Muslim lands, he laid but the more emphasis on our Lord's own words: "The things that are impossible with men are possible with God."

Of his own spirit in this work and the impression he made on students and others, something may be gathered from the following letters. Mrs. Henry W. Frost writes of his visit to Philadelphia:

> While in and near the city we had asked him to stay with us. One morning I met him in the hall, just starting for one of the theological schools. He stopped hesitatingly, and then said:
>
> "Mrs. Frost, would you have a little prayer with me before I go? I don't think they want me very much, as my invitation comes from quite a small group of students."
>
> We had prayer together, and I said, "Will you be back to luncheon, William?"
>
> "Oh, I don't know," was his reply: and then laughingly, "They may not want me any longer!"
>
> As a matter of fact he stayed all day and had a very interesting time.

A close friend heard him when he addressed the German department of the Rochester Theological Seminary. He wrote:

> After the address, he said that if there were any questions they cared to ask, though he would not promise to answer them all, he would be glad to try. Many questions followed—wise and otherwise—and I marvelled at his unfailing patience and complete lack of pride or self-consciousness, though he, the teacher, was probably the youngest of them all. During the months since I had seen him, a wonderful grace and sweetness had come into his life, but there was not one whit less of strength or humor.

---

[3]In proportion to the population, there were five hundred times as many ministers of the Gospel in the United States as there were ordained missionaries in China.

And a Yale classmate who attempted to draw him out on the subject of marriage wrote from New Brunswick:

> At the end of November, when Bill was here to give a talk in the Seminary, he came to my room and lay down on the couch, having caught a feverish cold. We talked over many matters. In a joking way I asked him when he was going to marry. He replied seriously that he thought it was cruel for a man who was going into one of the most difficult of missionary fields to ask any girl to go with him, because the woman always fared the worst, often succumbing when the man survived; that he had no intention of marrying—it would be wrong to the girl and would hinder his highest efficiency in the field he had in view. Bill's thorough-going decision on this question, which is so hard for many to settle, is another indication of his complete surrender of himself to the great work to which he was called.

Borden strongly approved the rule of the China Inland Mission with regard to outgoing missionaries, whether men or women, that they should remain unmarried for the first two years in China, so as to give undivided attention to the study of the language and have the best opportunity of becoming acclimatized and getting into contact with the people. It hardly needed the experience of the mission to prove that this was wise and helpful. To him it seemed common sense, and an obvious application of the Master's words: "Seek ye first the kingdom of God. . . ." His own problem extended, however, far beyond the two years. What about the period, long or short, when he would be practically homeless and exposed to hardships and danger? In one of his much-read books he had marked the lines from Meyer's *St. Paul*:

> Yes, without cheer of sister or of daughter,
> Yes, without stay of father or of son,
> Lone on the land and homeless on the water
> Pass I in patience till the work be done.

After his last meeting in December, concluding his three months' work in the colleges, he was dining with Dr. and Mrs. Angell in Rochester, and the latter wrote of being "deeply impressed with the fire and ardor of his faith."

As he sat at the table with us, talking of all he hoped to do for and in China, his face became glorified, his eyes shone with a light which only divine things can awaken. At the same time there was a poise, a dignity and balance which showed that his was not the mind of a fanatic. He was one who had counted the cost but never flinched for a moment.

"Those were fruitful months," wrote Mr. Fennell P. Turner, General Secretary of the Student Volunteer Movement. "William was used to leading students in many colleges and universities to give their lives to foreign missionary service. The last letter I received from him enclosed the 'declaration card' of a Student Volunteer who had signed it after his visit, and sent it on to him in Cairo. In years to come there will be missionaries in many fields who owe their decision, under God, to William's unselfish service during his last months in this country."

The leaders of the Volunteer Movement desired that the strong effective work should continue, but Borden had to leave in order to make arrangements before leaving for Egypt and felt that his departure should not be delayed. His work in the colleges ended December tenth, and it would have seemed natural to take the Christmas vacation at home and set out early in the new year. But the S.S. *Mauretania* was sailing on the seventeenth and was due to reach Port Said on New Year's Day. It meant only one week for packing and final preparations, but two or three weeks longer at the other end. Time was to Borden one of his most important stewardships. His mother did not hold him back, so it was a foregone conclusion. To him could never be imputed "the ungird loin and the untrimmed lamp."

One last contact Borden had with his Yale classmates was on November twenty-eighth. He ushered at Charlie Campbell's sister's wedding. They had a wonderful time and afterward, William packed and left for the city to spend the last few days with his mother.

He kept up his visits to the Yale Hope Mission through all his other engagements and had provided for its financial needs to be managed by Mr. Don O. Shelton of the National Bible

Institute. His love for the mission was just the same as when he had begun it six years previously with all the hopes and fears of a beginner. Bernhardt had been called to the prison reform work in Atlanta, Georgia, and his place was filled by Mr. and Mrs. William Ellis, Mr. Ellis having been saved from the depths of sin and misery in the bondage of alcohol.

"What has impressed you most since you came to America?" Dr. Henry W. Frost asked a much-traveled visitor.

Without hesitation came the reply: "The sight of that young millionaire kneeling with his arm around a 'bum' in the Yale Hope Mission."

William spent his last Sunday quietly with his mother. They went to church together in the morning, having no idea it would be their last time together, and on the following day he took part in the meeting held regularly in their home for prayer for the Muslim world. Several friends came to dinner that evening, including Dr. and Mrs. Frost and Mr. Shelton. William was leaving the next day, and by common consent the six men with whom he had been most closely associated in the work for God gathered in his room for a last hour of prayer and fellowship. Mr. Shelton wrote:

> We prayed that our beloved friend might be kept in safety throughout his long journey, and guided and upheld in all his ways. And then he prayed for us, and for the work we represented. He was so strong and vigorous in body and mind that night that we anticipated for him long and useful service. And in less than four months . . .

In the quiet of her room that night, weary and worn and sad, Mrs. Borden fell asleep, asking herself again and again, "Is it, after all, worthwhile?" In the morning as she awoke to consciousness, the still, small voice was speaking in her heart, answering the question with these words: "*God* so loved the world that He gave His only begotten Son. . . ."

"It was strength for the day," she said, "and for all the days to come."

From childhood, William's constant prayer with his mother had been that the will of God might be done in his life, and as he parted on the S. S. *Mauretania* it was still the same. Did it come back to him afterward, as it did to her, that their last petition together was that he might be taken to China and made a blessing among its Muslim millions—but only, "if it be Thy will"?

To the companion of his first long journey around the world, Mr. Walter Erdman, Borden wrote after leaving:

> It is not easy. There are many temptations and adversaries. Pray for me that I may have strength.

Among the Christmas letters opened in England was a faded sheet bearing a Christmas carol, with the refrain:

> Glory in the highest and goodwill to men.
> Peace on earth, peace on earth.

Beneath the verses and on the back of the page Mrs. Borden had written:

> Darling, a blessed Christmas to you! This is one of our old song-sheets used at home in Chicago years and years ago, when we were all together. Never did I realize so clearly the missionary meaning of Luke 2:10 "Good tidings of great joy which shall be *to all people*," as I did yesterday morning while sitting by your side in church.
>
> Just one word: I will never cease to be grateful for the rich blessing you have been to me, Dear, a comfort and a strength all your years to your devoted mother. What a rich New Year is unfolding before you! It was so beautiful having you with us in our little prayer-circle—just one more of the loving touches God has put to these last days.

PART IV

THE MISSION FIELD

Oh, let me live as if Christ died
But yestertide—
And I had seen and touched His pierced side:

I would rejoice as one who knows
How soon he rose,
To tread beneath His feet our unseen foes.

And I would work as if heaven bright
Were now in sight!
What if tomorrow bring that great delight!

—Selected

14

AS ONE OF THEM

1913

AGE 25

Having set my hand to the plough, my resolution was peremptorily taken, the Lord helping me, never to look back any more, and never to make a half-hearted work of it. Having chosen missionary work in India, I gave myself wholly up to it in the determination of my own mind. I united or wedded myself to it in a covenant the ties of which should be severed only by death.—Rev. Alexander Duff, D.D.

Cairo with its brilliant sunshine and lure of color and all its dust and heat was not new to Borden. He had visited it with Rev. Walter Erdman eight years previously, when they had traveled up the Nile to Assuan, seven hundred miles toward the heart of the dark continent. The colossal ruins of Karnak, the rock-hewn tombs of the kings, the temples of Thebes and Philae, the statues of Memnon and other remains of the ancient world stirred them profoundly.

Upper Egypt completely fulfilled Borden's expectations: the Nile itself, the contrast of the fresh green fields with the quivering sands beyond, the groves of date palms, villages of flat-roofed houses, camels with their dusky riders crossing the desert which stretches away as far as eye can see.

His first donkey ride in Egypt took him through the town

and out into the desert to the Bishareen encampment. The people were Sudanese, very different from any others he had seen. Wearing their hair in loose gimlet-curls, about eight inches long, the people were quite black and had clear-cut features.

Many Middle Easterners with very fair skin lived in Egypt besides the Egyptians. People of various shades of blackness as well as innumerable Arabs, Sudanese, and other races resided in Cairo.

But now it was as a missionary, not a traveler, that Borden was in Cairo—that great city that Dr. Maltbie Babcock wrote of as "a huge melange, and ecumenical potpourri, a huddle of the ends of the earth and the first and last of civilization."

It was not at Shepheard's Hotel, where he had stayed before, but at the Y.M.C.A. that he took up his quarters. Met at the railway station by Dr. Zwemer, he was soon introduced to the very heart of things in the missionary community. He found himself unexpectedly in touch with China as well, for a missionary from Hong Kong had discovered a Chinese student in El Azhar University. He spoke to Borden about the man on the day of his arrival. The lonely student, it appeared, was from the very province in which William was hoping to labor and was so cut off from his own country that he did not even know of the fall of the Manchu dynasty or the establishment of the new republic. Borden was eager to meet him, and almost the first entry in his journal was:

> Went to El Azhar with Mr. Gairdner. Met the only Chinese student there—the first Chinese Moslem I have ever seen, so far as I know.

What a world of interest that El Azhar proved to be, with its white-turbaned students, nine or ten thousand of them, from many lands, including Russia, Persia, North and Central Africa, Ethiopia, India, Arabia, and a couple of hundred professors (Sheiks), every one of whom had spent at least twelve years studying in the university itself! Old as it was, dating from the tenth century, and entrenched in Moslem bigotry and pride, it was not unaffected by the Christian influences at work around it. Only a few months before Borden's coming, an article had appeared in a religious paper in which one of its professors had written:

> Do not say that it is impossible to convert an Azhar Sheik and bring him to Christ, for with God all things are possible. Was I not a fanatical sheik in El Azhar, and was I not by God's grace converted? Today I pray that my fellow-sheiks may be won even as I was.

Numbers of students were attending the Monday evening meetings for Moslems that winter, at which Michael Mansour was speaking in great power. "Mighty in the Scriptures and in the Koran as well," he was attracting great crowds. A foreign missionary was always in the chair, to keep order, and Borden was soon in his element distributing Arabic Scriptures and tracts.

From the Y.M.C.A. headquarters it was no great distance to the American Mission where Dr. Zwemer lived, and where these Monday evening meetings were held, or to the compound of the Church Missionary Society at which a good deal of Borden's time was spent. For it was there that the students of the new study center took their courses in Arabic with the Rev. W.H.T. Gairdner, and in Islam and practical work with other missionaries. Eight or ten were taking the complete course and were attending Dr. Zwemer's lectures at the Y.M.C.A. and in the theological seminary. It was an earnest, vibrant circle, one to which Borden was soon giving great contributions. Mr. Gairdner found him "brim full of energy and hope, bringing a new element into our midst." Dr. Zwemer writes:

> I never saw a man come to Egypt with eyes more open to see the kingdom of God. Other men come to see the dead Pharaohs, to study history or join the great company of tourists all over the land, never once lifting their eyes to see the fields "white unto harvest." Borden had not been in Cairo two weeks before he organized the students of the theological seminary to attempt a house-to-house canvass with Christian literature for *the whole city* with its eight hundred thousand people.
>
> Here was a man with the frame of an athlete, the mind of a scholar, the grasp of a theologian as regards God's truth,

and the heart of a little child, full of faith and love; a man who was so tender in the relations of home-life that our children used to nestle upon his knee as if they had known him for years—and he a comparative stranger. . . .

Knowing that he had to learn Chinese, he came to Cairo to perfect himself in Arabic. Some people shrink from the foreign field, questioning, "Could I learn the language?" Here was a man who deliberately set before himself the task of learning not one but two of the most difficult languages in the world, before entering upon his life-work of declaring the unsearchable riches of Christ to Chinese Muslims. . . .

At Yale, at Princeton, in Cairo we see him digging deep, thinking deep and studying hard. . . . He did not import doubts to the Orient, he imported his great convictions of the eternal truth of God. . . . When he lived in Cairo he was a friend to the Coptic Christians and the Armenian Christians. He was a brother to the American missionaries and to the British missionaries. He attended the Scotch church and the American church, and at the last all sorts and conditions of Christians met together to do him honor.

Two weeks after his arrival in Cairo, Borden began to make arrangements to board with a Syrian family so that he might hear Arabic spoken as much as possible. One afternoon he accompanied Mr. Gairdner to a family that would accept Borden as a paying guest. The home was a surprisingly proper place with an order and cleanliness about it.

Borden began his first work for Muslims by distributing *khutbas*, little sermons in Koranic style published by the Nile Press. It required some courage to take the initiative with his two words of the spoken language, "Do you read Arabic?" and begin offering the booklets on the streets. But soon he found that it went very well. Only a few declined to take them.

One Monday night Borden went to his first service in Arabic held at the American Mission headquarters. A few weeks prior, a rumor was spreading that Mudbuli, a Muslim saint, had come out of his tomb and had taken refuge in the nearby Greek church. The more educated scoffed at the idea, but multitudes believed it, with the result that there was quite a riot taking form. Soon after, in a newly published Muslim book attacking Christianity, the author said that the resurrection of Christ was just like this Mudbuli affair, the story of a lot of silly women. He called attention to this matter as a joke. A Muslim convert, Michael Mansour, a former El Azhar student, went to the place where the book was printed and ordered five hundred circulars stating that he would answer the above statement, debating it with anyone who would come. This was the gathering that Borden and Dr. Zwemer attended. Expecting a riot, Mansour opened and closed the meeting with prayer. For nearly an hour he spoke holding their attention so that there was no disturbance and only one or two slipped out. It was a great triumph and, though Borden could only understand an occasional word, he was glad to have gone.

Another afternoon Dr. Zwemer and Borden went into the native bazaar to a book shop. It was near the Azhar, and they took opportunity to distribute the rest of the *khutbas* they had to students and others. Among the books they purchased were some Korans. When these were put in the bottom of the carriage there were strong objections from the driver and they had to be placed up on the seat beside the driver. The outing was relaxing and an enjoyable time for the two men to be together.

"Old Cairo is a bazaar," Dr. Babcock put it, "its narrow lanes overhung with cornice that almost touch; with awnings of rugs, balconies, grated windows through which secluded eyes peep; booths, like mere vestibules, with no windows or doors, their owners sitting, Turk-fashion, smoking, haggling, finally demanding your 'last price,' and following you often far along the way; with camels, donkeys, dogs, water sellers with their clanging brass cups, vendors of everything with cries to match, whips cracking like torpedoes; with Nubians, Abyssinians, Greeks, Copts, Arabs, veiled women in black silk balloons and high-heeled slippers, fellahin women with no veils but with tattooed skin and with babies on their backs, rug men and scarab-sellers, jewelers and brass-workers dragging you into their dens, beggars, cripples, children crying 'Baksheesh.' Oh, the streets of Cairo! The Mouski Bazaar no one who has seen can ever forget."

Every phase of missionary work in this cosmopolitan city interested Borden, and his sympathy and eagerness to learn were winning many friends. He was finding ways, too, in which he could wisely give financial help. At the Y.M.C.A. he was in touch with young men of various nationalities, whom he joined in sports as well as meetings. "He was a splendid young man, so healthy, mentally, morally and spiritually," wrote a Syrian friend with whom he was reading French. And the Christian Endeavor Meeting was long remembered at which he spoke on the topic, "Be a Christian: Why not?"

He laid himself out to encourage the Egyptian Student Movement. It was a gift of his that made possible the obtaining of much better quarters, including a room set apart for Bible study. Here the students of different institutions could meet in groups, one school having one night, and another school another.

"It is for this Bible-room that they are asking for a picture of Mr. Borden," one of their missionary friends wrote after his death. "They say that he was such a help to them, and his blessing is still with them in their work."

He was making time also for what in earlier days he used to call his "long-distance work"—letters to people with whom he had spiritual contacts. To Mr. H., for example, he wrote:

> I can sympathize with you in the matter of controlling your thoughts, for that is a thing we all have to fight for. You are right in saying we may commit great sins in our minds, though we do not do so outwardly. This is the view of sin which Christ gives us in the Sermon on the Mount, Matthew 5 and 6. However, I believe that in this as in all other things we can gain the victory by faith, through His aid, who was "tempted in all points like as we are, yet without sin." . . .
>
> The principle on which we want to work is to crowd out the bad with the good. If we merely seek to put away evil without replacing it with active good, we may find that worse things come in. I have been helped by the suggestion that when we are tempted to harbor evil thoughts we should at once think of Christ, or repeat some verse of Scripture—in this way spoiling the picture, so to speak, by letting in a flood of light. Our object must be to bring "into captivity every

thought to the obedience of Christ." 2 Corinthians 10:5.

Chief among his interest at this time was the distribution of the booklets in Koranic style. The idea had come to Borden early in his stay in Cairo. Writing about it to friends in New York, Dr. Zwemer said:

"How glad I am to hear of your good prayer meetings at the home of Mrs. Borden. Her son is a benediction to the work here, not only at the Y.M.C.A. but in both the missions. He is a spiritual power and up-to-date in his methods. At his suggestion we are starting the distribution of *khutbas* all over Cairo, the students of the theological seminary working with us."

It was a movement with prayer power behind it, and before long it was taken up by others in the missionary community, so that within six months of its beginning Mr. A.T. Upson, superintendent of the Nile Mission Press could say:

"There never has been a time in the history of mission-work at this center when there were so many inquirers."

The tract distribution led to many talks and endless possible openings for personal work. And who shall say how much further the results were carried since Cairo was the intellectual center of the Muslim world.

Although unconscious of the impact his earnest purpose would set in motion, Borden was giving every hour he could spare to his share in this work. The *khutbas* were brief, pointed discourses written by Mr. Upson and a converted El Azhar man, beginning with some passage from the Koran and leading up to clear teaching from the Bible. Borden appreciated their value. His idea was that there should be a shop-to-shop and, if possible, house-to-house distribution of these tracts. In his direct way he went to the seminary students and put the plan before them.

"I will pay for the *khutbas*, if you fellows will help me distribute them."

Wholeheartedly they did help, seeking to reach out with the gospel all through that great city of Cairo.

One afternoon Dr. Zwemer and a group of students went distributing to a fanatical part of the city. All went well for a

time, till they met an old man who wanted to know by whom
the tracts had been written. He was extremely disturbed when
he learned that it was a former El Azhar student who had
become a Christian. Dr. Zwemer, seeing that there was going
to be trouble, tried to get the students away and to disperse the
crowd by going into a shop. The crowd, however, waited outside and there was no way of escape. Finally, while the old
man continued his attack, they were all marched off to the
police station.

The officer looked at the *khutbas* and listened to the charge.
"Why," he said, "this is nothing but Christianity! You can read
about this any day." And he let them go.

The results were incredible! They were able to distribute
many *khutbas* right in the police headquarters, which would
have been inaccessible to them otherwise. They invited the
people to come to the Monday night meeting for Muslims, and
the man who began all the trouble attended the meeting as well.

Dr. Zwemer also began to run Christian notices in the daily
papers, inviting inquiry by letter or in person. He had received
several replies.

Borden purchased during this time a *tarboush*, a red fez,
to wear when he went to investigate Islam. It was remarkable
how effective such a slight change proved as a disguise. Many
of the natives wore European dress except for the hat. So when
he would put it on the natives weren't sure whether he was
"Christian" or not, but could be quite sure that he was not a
tourist. Borden found that not only the Egyptians took him for
a native but an American gentleman and his family who visited
Cairo about this time also did. The man roomed at Shepheard's
and one evening went out to see if he could find any preaching
going on.

"Only a few steps from the hotel," wrote Mr. J.S. Kimber,
"we found one of the mission halls. Near the door we saw a
man who, though he was wearing a fez, we thought might
understand English. While I was asking him one or two questions, my eldest son came up and said, 'I think I must have met
you at Princeton. Are you not Mr. Borden?'

"To my surprise the stranger said he was. He then gave us

all the information we needed, and volunteered to guide us amid the tremendous scenes of the celebration of Mohammed's birthday.

"Sometime later, we had been to hear Dr. Zwemer preach and had returned to the hotel, when I saw our friend in the lobby talking with a lady from the States, a young graduate from Mount Holyoke. I asked my son whether it would not be worth while for him to wait until the conversation was finished, and then to invite Mr. Borden to take a late dinner with us. After remonstrating a little about not being suitably dressed, or something of that sort, he consented. The dinner was pretty well under way when he joined us at table. He took his seat smilingly, and at once bowed his head in a reverent and silent 'blessing.' It was a beautiful sight, and one, as we remarked, not often seen at Shepheards's.

By this time Borden was living with the family to whom he had paid a visit with Mr. Gairdner. He had moved from the Y.M.C.A. to this Syrian home in the Shubra quarter, glad to be entirely among Arabic-speaking people. He wrote to his mother of the kindness of the Hassoon family and the comfort of his surroundings:

March 1, 1913

> While we do use a good deal of English, I hear Arabic spoken all around me, and am given lessons by various members of the family, at meals and any other time I wish. The flat is on the third floor of a house near the station, right by the tracks, but I do not mind that. I have a room facing north looking over other, lower houses, so I get quite a view. My room is rather small for what I have in it, but as I have the use of the dining-room and library as well, for study and writing, it does not much matter.
>
> The family consists of Mr. and Mrs. Hassoon, his sister, who goes by the name of Sitt (Miss) Paulina, and a niece, Sitt Negla. They are all very nice and most solicitous in trying to stuff me at every meal, claiming that I do not like the food unless I eat a great deal! It is really very good, and if I do not eat more it is simply because I have had enough. I have forgotten to mention the two little kiddies, Hilda and Vera. Vera,

the younger, has great big brown eyes, and is really very
cute. . . .

You ask if I am getting proper food, and I can honestly
say that I am. Some of the dishes are strange, and one or two
not much to my liking, but in the main they are excellent.
Some things which at home are luxuries are in common use
here, artichokes for instance, which we often have, cooked
in the most delicious manner. Then we have a good deal of
rice, which you know I like.

It was a time of excitement in the city, the Prophet's birthday and other subsequent festivities had arrived. The Dervish
dances were in full swing, attracting great crowds day and
night. For Cairo, as Borden was learning, is a center of the
secret organization known as the Dervishes, with its thirty-two
great mystic orders, "the very warp and woof of the Muslim
religion." While giving most of his time to the language, which
he wrote was "no afternoon-tea party," Borden was making a
study of this strange development in the life of the people
around him. The day he moved to the Hassoons he had "put
in some hard licks at Arabic," as he wrote in his journal, had
called on Mr. J. Pierpont Morgan at Shepheard's Hotel with
Dr. Zwemer, and was writing to his mother at night describing
some of their experiences.

Feb 20, 1913

I mentioned in a recent letter that we were going to see
some *zikrs* at the celebration of the Prophet's birthday. This
we did on Monday night, and it certainly was interesting,
though I fear I shall not be able to describe it at all adequately.
A large piece of level ground had been taken and tents erected
in a great square, an entrance being left at one side. Each of
the tents was assigned to a Dervish order, or some department
of the Government. The tents themselves were very attractive,
made of Oriental tapestries in rich red hues, and lighted with
glass chandeliers, each of which had a dozen or more big
candles. The effect was very brilliant. The floor in the center
of each tent was occupied by the Dervishes, who stood or sat
in a circle, or if there were many of them in two long rows
facing one another.

They all repeat more or less the same things—the name

of Allah, the Muslim Creed, the opening sura of the Koran,
or the ninety-nine beautiful names of God—but the accom-
panying motions differ. Some sit and move their heads, first
to one side, then to the other and down on the chest, swaying
their bodies at the same time, back and forth. Others stand,
bending from the waist in rhythmic motions. This was what
the Merganiyeh Order were doing as they repeated:

> La illaha il Allah,
> Muhammed rasul Allah.

At first they would bend slowly, then gradually increase the
pace till they were all going full speed, the leader keeping
time by clapping his hands or coming in with a solo refrain
in the marvelous way of intoning these fellows have. One
could not watch them without feeling the grip of the thing,
although knowing it was nothing but a deliberate attempt to
induce a state of ecstasy or auto-hypnosis. The Government
has put a stop to many of the worst excesses, so that now
these big functions are comparatively tame, and they seldom
go to the former extremes.

One man Mr. Swan pointed out to us is known as "the
Protestant Dervish." He preached repentance from sin, very
much like a Protestant minister, though, of course, without
any mention of Christ as the atonement and the One who
delivers from the power of sin. He had quite an audience,
which he managed much as an evangelist would at home—
getting responses from them and letting them ask questions,
first of all telling them good stories to get them in a favorable
humor. Dr. Zwemer calls him "The Billy Sunday of Islam!"

The next night, Tuesday, was the climax of the celebrations. . . . The Dervishes all paraded through the city, chanting and dancing, each Order making a company with its Sheik
riding on horseback. I followed them a long way, and saw
them as they came into the grounds at Abbasiyeh. It was really
very picturesque. . . . In the evening there was an immense
crowd, chiefly to see the fireworks—"an invention of the evil
one" that Mohammed certainly never supposed would come
to be connected with his birthday. The crowds hurrying
through the streets, the brilliant lights and all the excitement,
reminded me very much of the festival of Juggernaut in Madras.

It was not only as a student, however, but as a missionary that Borden went "zikr-hunting" as he called it. His companion was often a young German missionary named Straub, who was with him at the Study Center. The following description by Mr. Straub holds an interest all its own, describing as it does the last night of Borden's active service:

His zeal made me ashamed of myself. He always had his pockets full of *khutbas*, and lost no opportunity of distributing them. . . . He was greatly interested in getting acquainted with the national life and the doings of the Dervishes. For this purpose we went to Muslim festivals where *zikrs* were taking place, each wearing a red fez so as not to attract attention.

The last time we went together was on Thursday in Passion Week (March 20). It was the anniversary of the saint Abul Ela in Bulak. . . . What crowds of people were there to be seen—people of all classes and ages, men and women, people who were well and people who were sick! As these occasions partake of the character of national holidays, all sorts of amusements were going on. The illumination was truly fairy-like.

As our chief interest was in the various *zikrs*, we were drawn to one tent from which the sound of chanting reached us—"Allah, Allah!" For a long time we stood, side by side, watching the strange motions of the men who were swinging forward and backward in strict rhythm, shouting their "Allah, Allah." The tempo of these motions grew quicker and quicker; "Allah, Allah" sounded hoarser and hoarser, until finally nothing but heavy breathing could be heard. Several of the Dervishes fell unconscious to the ground. We noticed one man close beside us wrought up to the highest pitch, and saw foam gushing from his mouth. We, too, felt the excitement, and were full of pity for these poor, deluded people, whose way of worship was so unworthy. . . .

About midnight we started, arm in arm, for home, and had scarcely seated ourselves in the trolley when Mr. Borden took his remaining *khutbas* and handed them to those nearest to him.

His earnestness of spirit had been deepened by a startling occurrence of which he wrote to his friend, Dr. Inglis Frost, in March:

An event here in Cairo has saddened us all and made me realize afresh the heroism of the doctor in his everyday work. I refer to the sudden death of Dr. M. Pain of the Church Missionary Society, a man beloved by hundreds and filled with the Spirit of Christ. I only met him twice, soon after my arrival, and the next thing I knew he was dead.

I wish I could give you the full medical particulars, as you would be interested. As far as I could ascertain he was attending a patient suffering from spinal meningitis. The patient coughed in his face, and infection followed apparently. This took place on a Sunday, and the following Wednesday, about 5 A.M., he passed to the home above.

His funeral, attended as it was by a great crowd of natives and Europeans, was a most eloquent testimony to his loving faithfulness in serving his Master.

As they were leaving the cemetery Borden said to a companion: "Now we must work all the harder, for the time is short."

This made him appreciate his opportunities for learning the spoken language and coming into touch with the life of the people in the home of his Syrian friends much more. From a letter written by Mr. Gamil B. Hassoon, we have a glimpse of him through their eyes:

It is beyond power to describe his great zeal and diligence in studying the difficult Arabic language. But though he was so absorbed, so fond, so overwhelmed with his studies, he did not make Arabic his only aim. He looked to what was higher and nobler, and appointed a large portion of his time for reading the sacred Scriptures. His Bibles, and he had many of them, were all visited by his eyes. Many were the remarks on their margins made in his hand-writing, and the texts underlined, which showed that he had chosen them and probably put them into memory. His reading the Scriptures was not in the order of a daily duty. He read them because he loved them.

His life and deeds agreed to what he read. He loved everybody; and as a rule when you find one who loves like that you may be sure of his love to God. . . . In a conversation I had with him I found that he loved the Y.M.C.A. with a wonderful love and when our talk turned on the Arabic branch, his love to this seemed not less than to the other. I knew from him that he wanted to strengthen the Arabic branch by all the power he could, financially, morally and mentally, so that it might attain a level with the greatest European associations, and surpass them if possible. Many times he expressed to me his pleasure in the progress this branch had taken in the short time since it was organized, despite all obstacles.

His love to Orient and Orientals was a profound, true love. He was very pleased with many of our noble habits which he had not experienced before. He was very kindly sociable in our society, and in a few days, not exceeding the number of the fingers of one hand, he became one of us—Orientalist, with the full meaning of the word. He loved to communicate and mix up himself with us and we with him, preferring to change his long-accustomed habits and acquire our ways, so that he might prepare himself with what would agree with the taste of Orientals among whom he hoped to live. . . . The kindness and sociability God endowed him with were very great.

He denied himself, and had a special motto written on a paper in his pocket: "My Lord, enable me to conquer my will and overcome my desires." And he had another motto: "*not my will but Thine* be done."

What impressed me most was his strong faith. He did not think that there was anything impossible to do in the service of the Lord. In the books he and I read, we found that it is nearly impossible to enter into Tibet or Afghanistan, to bring the gospel to the Muslims there. But that fact was not to shake his faith. And he went further, believing that it is most possible that the gospel shall in a few years be preached in Mecca, the center of Islam itself. He loved to be where the fight is hottest. . . . The unoccupied fields of the Muslim world were his target, and all the time he was preparing himself for the evangelization of such fields. . . .

He was very fond of Muslims. Once he came home with a very pleased face.

"What is it that makes you look so happy?" I inquired.

He had met, he explained, two Azhar Sheiks, and stopped them by the way. They spoke to him in Arabic, something he could not understand. But he did all he could, and led them a long distance to Dr. Zwemer's house. Showing them the house, he said, "*Koll yom gomaa*," (every Friday). And he spent with them fifteen minutes by the roadside, using the few Arabic words he knew.

I asked him to repeat the Arabic he used, and we had great fun of it! But it was good enough to make those men understand that he wanted to gain them for Christ, and they parted with peace. To my full belief they went to Dr. Zwemer's on Friday. . . .

William had a winning look and an attractive spirit. He was meek and kind. My love to him is very great, and I remember every movement of his. . . . Although he was a rich man he denied himself the privileges of rich people, and lived as simply as any missionary could live. He was following the footsteps of Jesus.

Once a friend said to me: "Your guest is a millionaire."

"I do not know anything about his dollars," I replied.

When I came in I told Mr. Borden what I had heard, but he did not confirm it.

"People often mistake us," he said, "for the rich condensed milk firm that bears the name of Borden."

This put me into an opinion that he was not so rich, and I kept on treating him as a brother, not as to please a millionaire. I am sure he liked it that way. He was perfectly at home with that poor family of mine, and we lived together with great peace and love.

15

PERFECT THROUGH SUFFERING

April 1913

Age 25

Greater love hath no man than this . . . John 15:13

Dr. Zwemer had left for Jedda when a telephone call came from the Hassoon family on Good Friday, the twenty-first of March. It was to say that their guest was far from well. Mrs. Zwemer went over at once to the house by the railroad station, and found that Borden had seen the doctor already, who had told him to stay in bed. He had a headache and mild fever, but nothing apparently serious. He had been out a good deal in connection with his canvass of the city and with the *zikrs* that were going on, and might have contracted influenza, which was prevalent at the time.

Next morning the message was that he was better, so that it was a surprise to hear in the afternoon that he had been taken to the hospital. It was probably heat stroke, the doctors said, but no one could see the patient.

Easter Sunday came with all its gladness, but a shadow lay on the little missionary community, for Borden's place was empty. The hospital was five miles away, but after the morning service one of his friends went out to obtain fuller information.

"He was told," wrote Mrs. Zwemer, scarcely believing it possible, "that Mr. Borden had *cerebral meningitis*—which stunned us all. I chased the doctor from place to place, and saw him personally that evening, but he would not give any hope, only that Mr. Borden was no worse, and that serum had been injected into the spinal cord.''

So the blow fell, and that bright strong young life was suddenly challenged by suffering, if not death itself. Over the succeeding days, a veil of mystery hung—at least for those who were watching, near and far, with stricken hearts. As day by day the cables carried messages of alternate hope and fear, life seemed to stand still for many, and a great volume of prayer went up to God without ceasing.

One tragic element in the situation was that the relatives in America were unable to communicate with Mrs. Borden. She had already left with her younger daughter to join William in the Lebanon Mountains for the summer, sailing for Alexandria direct. They were not due in Gibraltar till the first of April, and efforts to reach them by wireless proved unsuccessful. Fortunately the older sister, who had just returned from India with her family, was still in London. Upon hearing of the illness she set out for Cairo at once, but it was the second of April before she could arrive.

Meanwhile Mr. Gairdner was visiting William daily, and Mr. Giffen of the American Mission obtained permission to see him once and again. The risk of infection was very serious, but Mrs. Zwemer could not keep away. Repeatedly she visited and prayed with him, bearing also all the burden of communication by letter and cable with those at home.

It was there in America that consternation and sorrow found their fullest expression. Miss Whiting, Mrs. Borden's sister, set aside everything to be in the Borden home in New York, answering letters and cables and keeping in touch with the large circle of enquiring friends. To her sister she wrote:

> I telephoned Mr. Frost and he came up of his own accord and remained until the following day at noon. He was most kind and could do a good deal of enquiring, writing notes, etc., while I had to be out. Mr. Delavan Pierson suggested a circle of prayer in which he and his wife would join; so Mr. Frost arranged this with Mr. Don O. Shelton.

Mr. Shelton telephoned me that hardly anything else had
been thought of for the day—all the workers of the institute
met with him in the morning, and the board of directors in
the afternoon, and that prayer would be continued strong and
steady until William's recovery was assured.

Laura telegraphed Mrs. H. who went at once to Dr. A.B.
Simpson, and there also daily prayer is offered. You, of
course, are as earnestly thought of as William. . . . I telephoned the Erdmans and telegraphed to many others, trying
not to leave out any one you would wish to be reached. Mr.
Frost wrote to Mr. Crowell . . . who would be the one to
speak to William's friends at the Moody Church. . . . Charlie
Campbell spent all one afternoon here. In many ways he made
William seem so near!

And then, sometime later:

It has been a blessing and even a joy to be here, where I
could come in touch with your friends and William's, and to
hear them speak the words of love and admiration and sorrow.
Even the men are not ashamed to be found in tears. No one,
no one can understand. They and we can only *know*. Dr. W.J.
Erdman showed the marks of the struggle in his face and
bearing as he said:

"It is the strangest, most mysterious working of the divine
providence I have ever experienced. The world had such need
of William!"

But in Cairo, in the shaded room at the Anglo-American
hospital, who shall say that there was question or mystery?
Suffering there was intense and prolonged, for William was
fighting the bravest fight of all his life. But he was not alone.
Had not his prayer from childhood been that the will of God
should be done in his life? There was no shrinking now. All
those Easter days, as he lay there, he could not but think of the
young doctor-missionary whose sudden call had come just in
the same way. A few weeks previously he had stood by that
newly made grave. What if, for himself too, the call had come?
No reserve, no retreat, no regrets had any place in William
Borden's consecration to God. With Adam McCall, the young
leader in the Congo, falling as one of the first missionary pioneers in that great region of central Africa, he might have said:

Thou knowest the circumstances, Lord. Do as Thou pleasest, I have nothing to say. I am not dissatisfied that Thou are about to take me away. Why should I be? I gave myself, body, mind and spirit to Thee—consecrated my whole life and being to Thy service. And now, if it please Thee to take me instead of the work I would have done for Thee, what is that to me? Thy will be done.

Among the friends who risked infection and were permitted to see Borden was his dear Syrian host. As soon as he stepped into the room, William, in spite of his great suffering, gave him a wonderful smile which became imprinted on Mr. Hassoon's memory. He tried to sit up in his bed for a time but very soon had to lay himself down again. Hassoon sat by his bedside for a short time and spoke to him with all the oriental and brotherly kindess he could master at that critical moment. He was greatly astonished that all William's sufferings did not hinder him from showing gratitude and love. Passing his hand over the feverish brow to wipe away the drops of sweat that stood there, he asked God to help and cure his friend. William smiled again and held his hand in his and pressed it very gently but warmly, in such a manner which made Hassoon feel his love. He was not able to speak much, but his eyes spoke, and transmitted to Hassoon's heart all that was in his heart and mind. And thus he left William for the last time.

Meanwhile Mrs. Borden and her younger daughter were nearing Cairo. Dr. Zwemer had returned from Jedda, where he had been enabled to witness for Christ within thirty miles of Mecca itself, and while in quarantine at Suez had received word of Borden's illness. From the second Sunday he was with him frequently, and even then there seemed hope, at times, that the patient's health would hold out. He recognized his elder sister who had come from London and with the nurses was doing all that love and skill could devise. He knew that his mother was expected, and asked for her in semi-consciousness, often saying: "Poor Mother! Poor Mother!" His work, too, was much upon his heart, for in delirium he talked about it constantly.

"This is the fifteenth day," Dr. Zwemer wrote early in April, "and he is slightly better tonight, although this morning the doctor had no hope. Mrs. Zwemer has done heroic work, both in visiting and in praying, as well as keeping in touch with Mrs. Borden by cable. The latter will be in Brindisi tonight and sails for Port Said tomorrow."

Three days later it was still with a glimmer of hope that he left for Port Said to meet the steamer. They had hardly cast anchor before he was on board, at five A.M., bringing what seemed good news to those who had so dreaded the arrival. In the relief of hearing that William was still living, the beauty of the spring morning and the novelty of all around them impressed itself upon the younger members of the party. They went ashore in small boats, everything seemed interesting and strange. The steamer was overrun with Arabs and Negroes of all descriptions. The harbor sparkled with light and bright colors. The ride from the water's edge to the railway station was fascinating, with the high palms, the veiled women, and the bright picturesque costumes of the Arabs.

They left by train at 8 A.M. and journeyed to Ismailia, following for many miles the banks of the Suez Canal. It was surprising to find the canal so narrow, and that the largest ocean steamers could pass through it. Almost at once after leaving the canal, the desert began—long stretches of sand with beautiful vistas far away, where the sand would look bright pink. Here and there would be a green patch, wherever water was to be found.

After a long time the Nile deposit began to appear—dark soil, very different from the sandy stretches, and getting blacker as they came into the cultivated land of Goshen. There, Arab life was all around them. Already in the desert they had seen camels wandering about, either alone or with a Bedouin in floating garments. Now they passed native villages—mud huts, people sitting around, children, veiled Muslim women, men loading camels, families riding on donkeys. After morning prayers and singing of hymns, they again each returned to their own thoughts about William.

At Ismailia, half-way to Cairo, a telegram was brought to them: "William not so well." Dr. Zwemer assured them that it had been like that all the time. Having reached a certain satisfactory level, he would drop below that level every second day, improving again the next day, so that they need not be overanxious.

They moved on. It was only a few stations farther that a second telegram came to Dr. Zwemer, right to the car. The word spoke of William's death.

Dr. Zwemer was the greatest comfort to Mrs. Borden and her young daughter Joyce. They reached Cairo at 1 P.M. William had passed away at 9 A.M.

The funeral had to be the same afternoon. His death was absolutely peaceful, without any struggle; he just simply stopped breathing. When Mrs. Borden herself could write, ten days later, she wrote:

> I do not want you to think of us as overwhelmed, for we are not. God's loving care and mercy have been evident on every side; and it has been a real joy to be in the place where William, in those few short weeks, became so honored and loved, and was so *happy*! The missionaries have all been most kind and thoughtful, and Dr. and Mrs. Zwemer wonderful in their loving sympathy and untiring efforts on our behalf. Dr. Zwemer has been son and brother in one. He loved William and could scarcely speak of him with unbroken voice. Dr. Gairdner, head of the language school where William was studying, visited him daily through all his illness, though it is considered dangerous to go near the sufferer. The nurses they tell me were devoted, and so were the Arab boy-attendants, night and day, keeping the flies away. As yet, it is all more like a dream than reality.
>
> But I wanted to tell you just one thing that you may not hear from anyone else: and that is that, when we saw him, it seemed as though William had been transformed into the very likeness of Christ, through suffering. I should never have known him, his beard and moustache had grown and the contour of his face was changed.
>
> We had been in doubt as to whether to go to the hospital to see him, altered as he would inevitably be; but thank God, we did—Joyce and I with Mr. Gairdner. We were told not to go near the bed, but that at a distance it would be safe. We approached a long, low building, standing right on the ground, so that it seemed as though we might be going to the tomb

itself, and the question "Who will roll us away the stone?" was almost on my lips. The door was opened, and immediately we were in the presence of all that remained here of our William.

I was so shocked at the change that I turned to beg Joyce not to look or to come in, but she had already done so, and said in the gentlest voice—afterwards, I thought, like the voice of an angel:

"But Mother, did you see how he looks like all the pictures of Christ—the crucified Christ?"

I looked again, and then indeed I saw.

One hardly dared speak of it to others, fearing it would be thought irreverent or fanciful. But I did mention it to Douglas in Mr. Gairdner's hearing, who quietly said:

"Yes, and you only stood at the threshold. If you had gone nearer you would have seen the resemblance more clearly."

I said that, standing there, I could only think of the words: "His visage was more marred than any man's."

"Yes," said Mr. Gairdner, "*His* visage—more marred than any man's."

It put such a holy, wonderful touch upon it all.

Perfect through suffering. It was as though we had been permitted a glimpse into the mystery of suffering, human and Divine, and had seen that through it God had, so to speak, given the final touches to William's life.

"Christ Jesus my Lord—for whom I have suffered the loss of all things, and do count them but dung, that I may win Christ, and be found in Him" (Phil. 3:8–9).

16

CROWN OF RIGHTEOUSNESS

His servants shall serve him: and they shall see his face. . .
Revelation 22:3–4

Far away in Kashmir, a Yale man, one of Borden's friends, was anxiously awaiting news. The mail arrived, bringing letters from home, and was leaving again in a few hours. In his solitude, Sherwood Day, the young missionary, wrote:

> Somehow, as I read your letter, I have a sense of victory and power that seems to bring that "Other Room" very near. Bill seems nearer and more gloriously living than he did at Yale or Cairo. . . . I cannot put on paper what his change of field means to me. He is the first of my friends whom I really loved, to be in that Other Place, and it makes that place very real. In fact, except for the pain to Mrs. Borden and his family, I am very happy in it all—a happiness that hurts, but one that rejoices in the victory of the thing. All victory is gained through pain, but it is a pain that spells joy—one of those strange things in life.
>
> I have absolutely no feeling of a life cut short. A life abandoned to Christ cannot be cut short. "Cut short" means not complete, interrupted, and we know that our Master does no half-way jobs. We must pray, now, that those to whom God wants this to appeal may *listen*. I am sure we can feel that He wants to use it, and that He counts on us to help.
>
> I am glad for Bill! In His immediate presence—no longer a clouded, imperfect experience, but a wholly satisfying one. What his life means to us all! I mean the life we knew, the

one he has finished, or the part he has finished. Put that loyalty, that staunchness, the quality for which weaker men called him "narrow," over against the "modern" line of things, and how Bill's life stands out! A splendid mind, a splendid body and a great soul—all handed over to the One who does *all* things well. It will mean more and more to me, as I try to do what my Master wants of me in this country, to know that Bill has finished his job and is just Over There. It all seems so near! I feel this is the greatest thing Bill ever meant to me— a sort of volunteering for another, shall we call it, "foreign field?"

Amid the flood of sorrow that flowed so deep and wide, *this* was the conviction that seemed to dominate all others.

"There could scarcely a greater loss befall us than this," wrote Dr. Robert E. Speer, in the first shock of grief. "William Borden was one among a million. There was no better among the younger men who have gone out from our colleges in the last ten years. It seems impossible that all that strength and devotion can have been taken away from the work of the Church down here. Evidently there are missionary undertakings of even greater importance elsewhere."

And to Mrs. Borden:

"You do not need to be told anything of your son's noble qualities of character, his simply rock-like faith, his loyalty that knew no limit, his remarkable abilities and above all the unreserved devotion to his Master. It is not possible to understand the providence that has taken him, except on the supposition that God has more important missionary work to be done elsewhere than it is possible for men to do here on earth, and that He needed your son in the ministry of those who serve Him day and night, and who look upon His face as they do service."

In Cairo, this note of triumphant faith was struck. It was so manifest in Mrs. Borden's life that the Syrian friend whose home seemed so empty could write of *her* help in *their* grief!

"I shall not forget that smiling, loving face of yours as long as I live. You were a great comfort to us, and we thank God for your coming to Cairo in the time of our trial."

From the hospital, the nurse who had been in charge wrote of "the memory of a brave man who had faced illness with fortitude and patience, and never grumbled or complained, and a brave mother who did not make other people suffer because she was heart-broken.''

"The funeral was very informal," wrote a friend who was with Mrs. Borden. "The Anglo-American hospital is beautifully located on the island of Gezira, in the midst of green meadows, palms and roses. From there we went to the American cemetery. How strange it was to have Arabs doing everything! A great many friends and missionaries were present, the Syrian gentleman, too, in whose family William had lived. They are lovely people, simply devoted to William. Mrs. Zwemer says that the conditions in their home were perfectly all right, and that there was no risk to health in being there. The food was good, and William was in no way tired or rundown when he contracted the disease.

"Mr. Gairdner read the service and the scriptures. Dear old Dr. Watson prayed, and so did Dr. Giffen and Dr. Zwemer. We sang 'Face to Face with Christ, My Savior.' I shall never forget it as long as I live. We stayed to the very last. The sun was going down, and the glow in the west was wonderful. They planted flowers on the grave, and it looked very beautiful."

A missionary friend who was present added:

> As we sang hymns during the service the Muslim gravediggers, standing a little way back, looked astonished, for it was all in such sharp contrast with the hideous and meaningless wailing which takes place at a Muslim funeral. Still greater was their astonishment as they watched the little company of native Christians weeping over the grave of a foreigner—one they had learned to love as a brother. Never shall I forget the feeling that came to us with our closing hymn:
>
> > "Sing it softly through the gloom,
> > While the heart for mercy craves;
> > Sing in triumph o'er the tomb—
> > Jesus saves, Jesus saves!"
>
> Our very souls were lifted out of their mourning into a glad and glorious triumph, and we could indeed say: "O death, where is thy sting; O grave, where is thy victory?"

Even the rough, varnished coffin could bring no pang to the mother's heart, different as it was from the casket that would have been provided at home. As she saw it lowered into the grave, containing all that was mortal of her son, a feeling swept over her, not of pain at the outward lack of harmony, but of wonderful joy and comfort in the thought of that entire life spent for Christ, scarcely a moment of it wasted.

The surroundings were very different in Princeton when the memorial service was held that gathered professors, students and friends in one common grief, but the note of victory was the same. Miss Whiting wrote:

> Some day you will read the true and appreciative words spoken at Princeton on Friday, but I wish you could have been there to feel the spirit of love and reverence. Dr. Charles Erdman said it was the most wonderful testimony and tribute he had ever listened to. . . .
>
> The day was ideal—Princeton in its first spring beauty; the hour, five o'clock, was perfect. Dr. Patton himself conducted the service in a way so dignified, reverent and affectionate that nothing more seemed needed. The chapel was nearly filled with students who had known William, and the service throughout was simple, strong, solemn, tender and triumphant. . . . As I listened, the whole of William's life seemed to sweep before me. There was not one word too much, nor undeserved. I marvelled that they had understood so truly and loved so deeply in the space of but three years.

Another memorial service in Princeton had a significance all its own. It was held in the little African Methodist Church, where Borden had taught in the Sunday school for two winters. The pastor learned in that meeting, for the first time, that Borden had been wealthy in his own right. They had loved him for himself: "For his deep consecration and unassuming Christ-like life. We never at any time asked him to contribute a single dollar. We asked him to teach, not to give." So the African children sorrowed for the loss of their friend.

At New Haven too, in the Yale Hope Mission, a touching service was held, the room packed with men of the very class Borden had sought to reach. One after another told of the new life that had come to them because of what Borden was and did, and one of the professors who had differed from him widely as to theological views, spoke of the house being filled with the fragrance of his love and service.

There and in the Moody Church in Chicago men were riveted by the story of what the grace of God had done in one they had known so well. A friend who was present wrote:

> 2 Chronicles 16:9 has been in my mind ever since Friday evening. God is ever intently looking for those whose hearts are right toward Him, that in and through them He may "show himself strong." And oh, the joy of his heart when He finds such a one! As William grew in knowledge of God, he lived up to that knowledge; as he learned more of God's will, he obeyed that will. He followed the Lord wholly. As with absorbing interest the great company listened to what God had wrought, one could not but feel that the fire of a holy purpose was lighted in the hearts of some of those young men and women.

In the Marble Collegiate Church, New York, crowded to its full capacity, the number of students present and their interest were also remarkable. Mr. Charles Campbell was among the speakers, and Mr. Delavan Pierson, editor of *The Missionary Review of the World*, who was impressed with "the strong note of triumph and praise to God." Mr. Don O. Shelton presided. The words of Mr. Hugh R. Monro had special weight as the testimony of a businessman well known in the great city:

> The thing that impressed me in my contact with William Borden was the fact that he was living the Christian life successfully. I suppose we all recognize the deep and abiding blessings of our discipleship. Some of us have a continuous consciousness of the abundant grace brought to us in Christ. Yet even in advanced Christian experience there is often an overpowering sense of insufficiency and failure, so that we are constrained to confess and bewail our weaknesses. Where there is triumph in one direction there may be failure in another. But more than any other young man I have ever known Borden seemed to have continuous victory. His life was so truly under the control of divine power that it breathed the spirit of the conqueror. It was an imperial spiritual life.
>
> To myself there comes a new sense of assurance as I think of it, because I recognize that this overcoming life was not lived in the strength of any innate ability or natural gifts. It

was the grace of God in him that made his life victorious and
such a benediction to those with whom he came in contact.
The same resources are available to your faith and to mine,
so that while his life is a rebuke to the poverty of our spiritual
experience it is a summons also to a closer following of the
Savior. . . .

So it was in other memorial services: in Japan, Korea, India
and South Africa, for the circle touched by this young life was
practically worldwide. A friend in America wrote, "All the
papers in the country seem to have told about William," and
another, "I never heard, on all sides, such regret and sorrow
expressed over the death of any young man. . . . Surely you
must feel the volume of prayer that is rising for you from many
hearts."

"How strong his influence is, even in this remote corner!"
wrote a missionary to Korea. "Many of our Christians know
of him and his faithful consecration to the Lord. So he continues
to live here below in many souls made better by his example."

And from Cape Town came the following:

"You have no idea, Mrs. Borden, what William's life has
meant to the South African students who knew him at Princeton, and what it means just now to the whole Dutch Reformed
Church out here. Next Sunday the story will be told to the
children practically throughout the whole Union of South Africa, in hundreds of Sunday schools."

More permanent records, also, carried the message of his
life far and wide, in several languages. Two of his own ad-
dresses were put into Arabic by Dr. Zwemer's arrangement,[1]
who wrote of the booklet: "It will make a fine message. I am
calling it in Arabic: *Two Questions by a Young Man to Young
Men*."

A sketch intended especially for Muslim readers was prepared by Dr. St. Clair Tisdall and published in English and in
Arabic. A little later it was translated into Persian and Hindus-
tani and circulated by the thousand, then into Dutch and
Chinese. Of the latter translation made by a master of that

---

[1]*What it Means to be a Christian* and *The Price of Power*.

language,[2] Mr. F.H. Rhodes of the China Inland Mission said:

As the first Chinese booklet published for free distribution among Muslims in China, this story of Borden's life marks a distinct advance in bringing the gospel to these neglected millions. Requests for the book have come from practically all the districts where missionaries are in contact with Islam, and some even from Muslims themselves who have heard of the memorial. Thirty-five thousand copies have been put into the hands of Muslims, and as they are now being read, passed on to others and carried farther into regions where Christ is not named, we trust that the number who will hear the message will be much larger than the number published. Already the story seems to have opened the way for several missionaries to get into closer touch with the followers of Islam in their fields.

Thus in nearly every province of China proper, in Manchuria and far out on the great road across central Asia, Borden's love to Christ was the means of making known the love of God in Christ to followers of the Prophet. It was a wonderful ministry, wider possibly than he might have accomplished in person, and its outcome who shall tell?

A sketch of Borden's life by Dr. Charles Erdman appeared in *The Missionary Review of the World*, and was so requested that it had to be published separately in pamphlet form. Yet another, written from the point of view of the college student, came from Charles Campbell, with all the freshness of a classmate's understanding and appreciation.

A volume might be filled with the letters that flowed in— letters from leaders in the front rank of Christian activity, as well as from fellow students and friends of his own age. From the National Parliament in Peking and the House of Commons in London, from great city churches, Oriental universities and lonely mission stations came the same testimony.

"Mr. Borden has become a national character in his life and influence," said a leading man in Chicago. "It gratified me to hear him speak as he did," wrote Dr. J. Timothy Stone,

---

[2] The Rev. F. W. Baller.

"because he is careful as to what he says, and views everything with a broad and real justice."

From the Fifth Avenue Presbyterian Church in New York, Dr. Jowett wrote, "His life just now is standing before the American people like some perfumed flower from the garden of God."

"Apart from Christ, there is no explanation of such a life," said Professor Charles Erdman at Princeton.

"I know of no young man in this country or in England," wrote Dr. R.A. Torrey, "from whose life I expected greater things. But God has His own way of carrying out His purposes. He has some larger plan of usefulness through your son's departure than could have been realized by his remaining here."

"The loss is wholly inexplicable," came in a letter from Dr. Charles R. Watson of Egypt, "but the thing which forbids doubt or criticism is, from the human side, William's own spirit of perfect surrender. He had given himself to his Lord for life or for death, and where he trusted we cannot but share his truth."

On his return from Asia, Dr. John R. Mott said that missionaries in every part of the world bore testimony to the influence of the life of William Borden, and that at the student conferences that summer (1913), no appeal was being used with such power as the story of his consecration.

"Many young men live stronger, purer, more yielded lives," wrote a fellow-student, "because of the life your boy lived and because of the death he died. You cannot *hear* of them all. You will know some day. The name of Will Borden was more used than any other during the recent great Convention in Kansas City. Japanese students remarked that the investment of life as Borden invested it was the greatest of all investments. The memory of such a son must be a blessing. I am glad he lived *and lives*."

"At Bryn Mawr," a female friend wrote, "when Dr. W.J. Erdman preached here in May, he told of William as an example of the Spirit-filled life—and oh, Mrs. Borden, it was a marvelous witness! I know it must have struck deep into many hearts."

Dr. Henry W. Wright, of Yale University, said, "No undergraduate since I have been connected with Yale has done so much for Christ in four short years as Bill did. I feel very lonely trying to work without his visible presence to cheer and inspire me."

"William's life has touched many of whom you have never heard," Mrs. Walter Erdman wrote from Korea, "and no one can measure its influence. As for Walter, you can hardly realize what a blow it has been to him. It is the loss of a cherished brother, rather than a friend." And the Rev. Walter Erdman himself:

> We have been praying tonight that you may be comforted in the assurance that the love of God does *not* change, even when our understanding is baffled by His acts, and that our lives may be purified and made stronger through the inspiration of William's friendship and love and his loyalty to Christ. I learned more things from William about simplicity of faith and steadfastness of purpose than he did from me, during the year we were together while he was still a boy, and the memory of our comradeship will be dearly prized until we meet again. . . .
>
> I have been thinking more and more, since the news came, that the length of time God permits us to stay here is not related to a certain amount of work He wants us to do, so much as to a certain closeness of relationship to Himself He wants us to attain. Some of us who are less useful, perhaps, are allowed to live on longer that we may learn more and be perfected in understanding. And as for the mystery of the interruption of such a work as his was and promised increasingly to be, while there is no explanation now, I like to think that it is *not* interrupted, but that as he desired to serve so he will be permitted to serve, only with higher powers. I think of him as still working for Muslims in some relation to the proclamation of the gospel.

Mr. Fennell P. Turner of the Student Volunteer Movement wrote of the fellow-worker he had loved:

> Few men plan their preparation with such care and earnestness or carry out their plans with such faithfulness. What great things we expected of him, and how he is missed! But

we have this assurance: the life so truly given to God was His life and the work William was preparing to do was His work. On *His* heart rests a far greater burden for the Muslims of China than we can possibly feel. He will not permit His work to suffer or be hindered because His servant was not allowed to enter upon it as he had planned.

And a classmate who had preceded Borden to China wrote from Nanking:

> Somehow, already, I seem able to look down the years a bit and see, not one, but *many* giving their all to the Master to take up the work for Muslims here in China which William had planned to do. Just as Keith Falconer and Horace Pitkin did more even in death than in life, may we not believe that God will, out of seeming loss, get great glory to Himself and call many to fill the breach? William was taken while doing with great joy and enthusiasm the work to which God had called him. When my call comes, I pray that I may be found doing my Lord's work with like faithfulness and devotion.

In Cairo, Dr. Zwemer spoke in the place and among the friends Borden had last loved. There in the American Mission were gathered representatives of all forms of Christian service from throughout the city, Americans, Europeans, and men wearing the fez and the white turban of the Azhar student. Few leaders had influenced Borden more than Dr. Zwemer, and none could have had truer insight as he spoke at that memorial service from the words: "I have fought a good fight, I have finished my course, I have kept the faith" (2 Timothy 4:7).

One of the great characteristics of this life we mourn and in which we rejoice is that our friend and brother was a soldier, every inch—a soldier of Jesus Christ. Those who knew him best knew that he was fighting, and now he "has fought."

He won that greatest victory of all, the victory over himself. Charles Kingsley, who knew that life was not a bed of ease or a garden of roses, wrote:

> "The very air teems thick with league'd fiends;
> Each word we speak has infinite effects;
> Each soul we pass must go to heaven or hell. . . .
> Be earnest, earnest, earnest—*mad* an thou wilt:
> Do what thou doest as if the stake were heaven

And this thy last deed ere the judgment day."

And Borden was earnest. No one could say of him that he trifled with the thing men are trifling with all around, the great talent of life.

He won the victory over his environment. By some the victory has to be won over poverty; by others over heredity, or over shame and temptation; but Borden won the victory over an environment of wealth. He felt that life consisted not in "the abundance of things a man possesseth," but in the abundance of things which possess the man.

He won the victory in great measure over sin and temptation. There is not a young man living in America today who has not to fight a deadly battle for character. Borden fought and won—for two reasons: he always carried his sword and looked up for strength. He was a man of the Bible, as his Greek Testament and the Bibles he used for study and devotion show, and he was a man of prayer. . . . Even in the smallest details of life he looked up for wisdom and strength.

Another great thing that comes into a man's life is "urgency." At college as well as here in Cairo, Borden felt the call of urgency, and to him this was linked with thoughts of the Muslim world. I found underlined in his Testament *I must work the works of Him that sent me while it is day*.

The real secret of this full-orbed life was that, like St. Paul, Borden could say, "I have kept the faith." How many men in these days—men at the beginning of their ministry, or in pulpits, or at the end of their service—have to cry, "God knows, I have lost the faith." Borden held to the Bible. He believed it from cover to cover. His faith had been tested, for he had met destructive criticism in his college course. He had a grasp of the oracles of God, and to us it was a great joy to see that *belief in the Book* had made him a missionary.

He gripped the essentials; he had no shibboleth; his was no narrow creed. This gathering is indicative of his wide fellowship. His Egyptian brethren could never have told to which regiment he belonged in the army of God. He was too big a man to wear the distinctive colors of any regiment. He kept the faith—but he did not keep the faith to himself. Ask the men who met him.

"Henceforth there is laid up for me a crown of righteousness." He now wears the crown of life and glory. "O God, to us may grace be given to follow in his train!"

Only today I was reading in *Pilgrim's Progress* of the death of Valiant for Truth:

" 'My sword I give to him that shall succeed me in my pilgrimage, and my courage and strength to him that can get it. My marks and scars I carry with me, to be a witness for me that I have fought His battles who will now be my rewarder.' . . . So he passed over, and all the trumpets sounded for him on the other side."

17

LEGACY OF A STEWARD

Who is there tonight who can always see the shadow of the Cross falling upon his banking account? Who is there who has the mark of the nails and the print of the spear in his plans and life, his love and devotion and daily program of intercession? Who is there who has heard the word of Jesus and is quietly, obediently, every day, as He has told you and me, taking up his cross to follow Him?"

—Rev. Samuel M. Zwemer, D.D.

Two remarkable wills were probated within a few days of each other in the spring that followed Borden's sailing for Egypt, one his own, made in the fall of 1912, and the other that of J. Pierpont Morgan, who died possessed of almost a hundred million dollars. Though a devout believer, who prefaced his will with the statement, "I commit my soul into the hands of my Savior, in full confidence that having redeemed it and washed it in His most precious blood, He will present it faultless before the throne of my Heavenly Father," Mr. Morgan at the age of seventy-five left little more than half as much to the work of God as William Borden left at twenty-five.

Mrs. Borden and her sister, going over William's check books, found that during the three years at Princeton Seminary he had given away about seventy thousand dollars to Christian work, as far as the stubs in hand showed. This was a surprise to them, as he never referred to his giving.

Perhaps nothing is more distinctive than the way in which people do kindnesses, especially in the matter of financial help. Easy as it may seem, it is one of the most difficult things to give helpfully. Borden's way was characteristic.

"Few Christians of ample means," said Mr. Hugh Monro, "succeed in realizing such a degree of detachment from their possessions as to remove all sense of restraint in their dealings with their fellows of every station. Borden had learned the art of administering wealth on a large and generous scale, without a trace of self-consciousness and with complete self-effacement."

Charles Campbell, Borden's close friend, recalls: "Bill always followed the injunction, 'Let not thy left hand know what thy right hand doeth.' He insisted that not even his initials should appear when a list of benefactions was published. It almost seemed to irritate him if he was found out. His best friends never knew even a small percentage of the gifts he was making. Many surprising incidents would come to light if all who had been helped by him could be induced to tell their stories. Bill's check-books show how little he spent for himself and how much he was doing for others."

Standing in the doorway of their Princeton home, Borden's love of cars was awakened one day as a fine automobile flashed by.

"Gee!" he exclaimed, "Wouldn't I like a car like that!"

"Why do you not get one, William?" asked the friend who was with him.

"I cannot afford it," was the unexpected reply.

His money was not his own, and there were always ways in which it was needed for the Master. A Princeton classmate wrote:

> I have been told that he felt one of his temptations was to own a car. He never purchased one, because he thought that for him it would be an unjustifiable luxury. I remember one Saturday afternoon in New York going with him to the automobile show in a hall at Madison Square Garden. He knew all the various makes, and pointed out to me the advantages

of the different cars. But we left the hall to take dinner at the Y.M.C.A. and spend the evening down at the Katherine Slip and Doyer Street Missions. And he had filled his pockets and mine with copies of St. John's Gospel to use in personal work.[1]

Mrs. Borden felt that William's real reason for the stand he took about a car was that he deprecated the luxury seen in the lives of so many Christians. He did not feel justified in using his money, which he held distinctly as a stewardship, for any such purpose. All the time the Borden's lived in Princeton, Mrs. Borden felt he was longing to have a simpler way of living.

Though separated from his home church a great deal the last ten years of his life, Borden never lost his heart interest in the work of the Lord in that place. He inaugurated and supported in his church the largest daily vacation bible school in Chicago, a program bringing more street children into their Sunday School and services than any other movement they undertook.

He was the largest giver to their street preaching program, to the Sunday school, and to the general expenses of the church during the last years of his life, and he left to that church one hundred thousand dollars, realizing the wonderful opportunity it had as a downtown church to "preach the gospel to every creature" within the reach of its influence, in that teeming city of thirty different nationalities.

He believed that the church could do a great foreign missionary work right in Chicago. During his lifetime he made use of his money in world-wide ministry, yet so quietly that his left hand did not know what his right hand was doing. After William's departure, however, his statesmanlike grasp of the problem of the evangelization of the world in this generation became apparent, for he bequeathed the major portion of his inheritance, about one million dollars, in four nearly equal parts, for the purpose of preaching Christ—one-fourth to be used in Chicago, another quarter in other parts of the homeland, the third portion in China, and the remainder in other foreign countries.

---

[1]Rev. L.C.M. Smythe of Charleston, S.C., a missionary to Japan.

A Chicago friend gives a picture of the type of man Borden was:

> This was William Borden: quiet but powerful; saying little but doing much; rich but self-denying; humble in spirit but imperial in purpose; a general in organization, but always willing to be a private in service. He declined our urgent invitation to preach in the Moody Church, on the ground that he was not capable, but he was not ashamed to tell of his faith in Jesus on the street corner. His heart went out to the uncared for, Christless millions of Kansu, but he did not overlook the worthy widow, orphan and cripple in the back streets of Chicago, as some of us well knew. He was intent upon seeking to win for Christ and His service the young men of our colleges and universities, and to this end the last months of his life in America were given, but that did not prevent his thinking of, praying for and giving to the care of little children and the aged.

His provision for the China Inland Mission manifested the same breadth of mind and tenderness of spirit.

"I do not like to speak of his money," Dr. Henry W. Frost said in this connection. "We seldom thought of it while he was with us. But I refer to his bequest to the mission that I may mention his desire with regard to a portion of it. He asked that a hundred thousand dollars might be invested in order that the interest upon it should be used for aged and infirm missionaries. A young man of twenty-four thinking of and providing for old and infirm missionaries! Could anything be more far-reaching in thought and sympathy?"

When the provisions of the will were made public, the Rev. E.Y. Woolley, acting pastor of the Moody Church, wrote to Mrs. Borden:

"What a remarkable document it is! The *Chicago Tribune* has the best report of it, which no doubt you have seen. Its testimony to Jesus Christ as Lord and Savior will do untold good. And what noble bequests! The whole world will be touched for Christ by your son's life and act. . . .

"Mr. Borden's magnificent gift to the work of the Lord in and through the Moody Church has inspired our people to do and dare greater things for His glory. One very poor and very sick woman, who has been praying and giving for a new church for several years, was transported with praise to God when she heard of this."

The Rev. Charles R. Erdman, D.D., of Princeton Seminary, in his published sketch of Borden's life, *An Ideal Missionary Volunteer*, made the following statement with regard to his will:

> It is an extraordinary document, not only in view of the actual bequests which it provides, but also because of the spirit it manifests of loyalty to Christ and devotion to the work of world evangelization. It is in itself a missionary appeal. Its largest provision is for the China Inland Mission, in connection with which the donor had expected to serve and on whose Council he held a place. For the work of this mission he bequeathed the sum of $250,000; and with unique sympathy and thoughtfulness for one so young, this was added: "I suggest that $100,000 of this amount be invested, and the income thereof be used for the support and maintenance of missionaries and other workers connected with said Mission who through age or infirmity have become incapacitated for active service in the mission field or at home, and who are in need of and deserving of aid."
>
> The sum of $100,000 was left to the National Bible Institute of New York; and like amounts to the Moody Bible Institute of Chicago, and to the Chicago Avenue Church; $50,000 each was given to Princeton Theological Seminary, to the Board of Foreign Missions of the Presbyterian Church, U.S.A., to the Board of Foreign Missions of the Presbyterian Church, U.S. (South), to the Board of Foreign Missions of the United Presbyterian Church, and to the Chicago Hebrew Mission; and $25,000 each to the Nile Mission Press, to the American Bible Society, to the Chicago Tract Society, and to the Africa Inland Mission. Of the remaining estate, the China Inland Mission and the three Presbyterian Boards were made the residuary legatees. . . .
>
> Another provision suggests that William Borden had a definite and adequate *missionary message*. Nothing troubled him more than to see men of culture, ability and devotion planning to undertake missionary work while they were evidently ignorant of the great essential truths of the gospel. He therefore requested that his money should be used in the support of only such men as held absolutely to the deity of Christ

and His vicarious atoning death for sinners. "It is further my desire," so runs the will, "that the said bequests hereinbefore made be used and disposed of in accordance with the following recommendations by me, to wit: That each of said bequests be used for and in connection with missionaries and teachers who are sound in the faith, believing in such fundamentals as the doctrine of the divine inspiration and authority of the Scriptures, the doctrine of the Trinity, including the deity of Jesus Christ, and in the doctrine of the atonement through the substitutionary death of our Lord Jesus Christ."

So statesmanlike a leader as Dr. John R. Mott was profoundly impressed with the quality of this young man's life and giving, as may be seen from the following letter to Mrs. Borden:

My association with William has given me a keen appreciation of the value of the service which he accomplished for Christ and His kingdom by his life, by his witness, by his gifts, and by his activities. It has been on my mind for some time to write you to express my personal conviction as to the marked contribution which he made to his generation within the sphere of his influence. He exerted a great influence in the direction of the conservation and expansion of the spiritual life of our colleges. This he did through his constant and helpful work in the Christian Association and Volunteer Movement during his student days, as well as in his many personal relationships.

The sincere solicitude he manifested that the central points of our Christian faith might be preserved in purity and reality was one of the strong personal factors of which we have not had too many in resisting the movements and influences tending to disintegrate faith. The manner in which he sought to bring to bear the vital and superhuman power of Christianity upon the needs and problems of individuals and of society both during his college and seminary days was simply splendid. From the time I became acquainted with him as an undergraduate until I last saw him, his dominant ambition seemed to be the world-wide spread of the kingdom of Christ. He did as much as any young man whom I knew to help realize the watchword of the Volunteer Movement: *"The Evangelization of the World in this Generation."*

There is another aspect of his life and work which impressed me very deeply, and that was his attitude and practice with reference to money. I have read many comments in religious periodicals of different countries regarding the disposition which he made of his estate in his will. Without doubt he set an example to the rapidly multiplying number of wealthy young men and women; but to my mind even more instructive than his final will was his life-habit as a young man with reference to his money. This to my mind was truly remarkable. As you know, I was brought into the most intimate relations with him on this side of his life, in connection with different Christian enterprises which he so generously helped to promote.

I would like to mention a few things which characterized his giving. It manifested foresight and rare discernment. I have seldom met a person who showed such penetration of mind in estimating the worthiness of causes, in seizing opportunity at the flood and in anticipating results. His conscientiousness in the use of his money was always apparent. His chief concern seemed to be that of not making simply a good use of the money but the very best use of it. One was conscious of the fact that he regarded himself as a trustee and in no sense a proprietor.

His thoroughness in investigating objects was nothing less than remarkable. I have known a great many wise donors, but only one or two others who employed as thorough processes in seeking to estimate the worthiness of causes and the wisest ways of helping. He had evidently chosen a few clear guiding principles to help him determine his duty as he faced opportunity to relate his gifts to the plans of the Kingdom. These principles were such as led him to devote his money to promoting the most vital spiritual processes.

These traits, together with his prayerfulness in determining what to do with his money and in following his gifts, and above all his wonderful generosity, mark him out as a model to the young men of his generation to whom God may have entrusted financial power.

18

THE UNFINISHED TASK

What though he standeth at no earthly altar,
Yet in white raiment on the golden floor,
Where love is perfect and no footsteps falter,
He serveth as a priest for evermore.

—Selected

In far away Kansu, some new influence was in effect. After Borden's death a great change came over the province to which his life was given, so that far from being what it was, one of the most barren fields in China, it began to become fruitful. Wonderful things happened there, right in the midst of that great Muslim population, that put to shame our small expectations and little faith.

Its geography was critical. That part of China was one of the most charged with highly explosive political powers. Communism as well as Islam and the most bigoted forms of idolatrous worship had to be reckoned with. Men, women, and children came to the Savior who had never had a chance to hear of Him before.

God needs lives that count—the world needs them. China needs them and the Muslims of central Asia need them, waiting in age-long darkness.

From many a mosque there comes the call to prayer;
I hear no voice that calls on Christ for light—
But still I wait
For the messenger of Christ who cometh late.

206

COMMISSIONED

"As the Father hath sent me, even so send I you."—John
20:21

Out from the realm of the glory-light
Into the far-away land of night,
Out from the bliss of worshipful song
Into the pain of hatred and wrong,
Out from the holy rapture above
Into the grief of rejected love,
Out from the life at the Father's side
Into the death of the crucified,
Out of high honor and into shame
The Master willingly, gladly came:
And now, since He may not suffer anew,
As the Father sent him so sendeth He you.

Henry W. Frost, D.D.